GOVERNING
CANADA

Michael Wernick

GOVERNING

A GUIDE TO THE

CANADA

TRADECRAFT OF POLITICS

on
point
PRESS

VANCOUVER | TORONTO

30 29 28 27 26 25 24 23 22 21   5 4 3 2

Printed in Canada on FSC-certified
ancient-forest-free paper (100% post-consumer recycled)
that is processed chlorine- and acid-free.

Library and Archives Canada Cataloguing in Publication

Title: Governing Canada : a guide to the tradecraft
of politics / Michael Wernick.

Names: Wernick, Michael, 1957- author.

Identifiers: Canadiana (print) 20210300639 |
Canadiana (ebook) 20210300655 | ISBN 9780774890533 (softcover) |
ISBN 9780774890540 (PDF) | ISBN 9780774890557 (EPUB)

Subjects: LCSH: Political leadership—Canada. | LCSH:
Canada—Politics and government.

Classification: LCC JL65 .W47 2021 | DDC 320.971—dc23

Canadä

UBC Press gratefully acknowledges the financial support for
our publishing program of the Government of Canada (through
the Canada Book Fund), the Canada Council for the Arts, and
the British Columbia Arts Council.

Printed and bound in Canada by Friesens
Set in Candara and Utopia by Artegraphica Design Co.
Substantive editor: Lesley Erickson
Copy editor: Robert Lewis
Proofreader: Alison Strobel
Cover designer: Will Brown

On Point Press, an imprint of UBC Press
The University of British Columbia
2029 West Mall
Vancouver, BC, V6T 1Z2
www.ubcpress.ca

CONTENTS

1

A VIEW
FROM THE DESK
IN THE CORNER

If you visit the East Block on Parliament Hill, you will pass through a room that used to host Cabinet meetings before they were moved to the Centre Block and then to the West Block, where they now take place. In the corner you will see a small wooden desk, reserved for the Clerk of the Privy Council, who is the Secretary to Cabinet, a role that goes back eight centuries to English kings. In Canada, there are still desks or tables off to one side for the clerk and for senior staff in the Prime Minister's Office (PMO) and in the Privy Council Office (PCO), even when Cabinet meets outside of Ottawa.

I had jobs that placed me at one of those desks for part of the mandates of four very different prime ministers. I served as the deputy secretary to Cabinet from 2003 to 2006, a period that encompasses the later days of

Jean Chrétien's final mandate, all of Paul Martin's government, and the start-up months of Stephen Harper's tenure. I returned to the PCO eight years later as deputy clerk of the Privy Council for the last year of Stephen Harper's government and the early months of Justin Trudeau's tenure. In January 2016, Prime Minister Trudeau asked me to serve as the twenty-third Clerk of the Privy Council – the real "desk in the corner" – a job that I held until the spring of 2019. In other roles in earlier times, I was often in the room at a Cabinet meeting or a Cabinet committee meeting as a PCO staffer, when I worked at Canadian Heritage, or as the deputy minister at the department that was then called Indian and Northern Affairs, accompanying one of my ministers who was presenting an agenda item. By my rough estimate, I was in that room 250 times.

There are now 38 million Canadians, and only a small number are chosen to sit at that Cabinet table, even fewer to sit in the prime minister's chair. I vividly remember the buzz the first time that I strode up the path to the Centre Block and had to show my freshly issued ID card a few times in order to walk up the stairs and into the Cabinet suite. It was 1987. I never lost that sense of anticipation, responsibility, and privilege over the next thirty-two years. I hope that this book reflects some of those feelings.

This book is not a prescription for reform or for how things ought to be. Nor should it be read as a defence of the status quo. Others can take up those causes and battles.

This is a book about governing – more specifically, about the tradecraft of governing. My view is that regardless of ideology or personality, there are some elements to governing that, approached mindfully, can be learnable skills. This book attempts to distill and to make accessible to a wider audience ideas that I have often been asked to convey behind closed doors or in private conversations. It is focused on "how it works," or at least on how it has worked in my experience.

THREE DECADES

This experience stretched over three decades and several governments. Currents of fortune, timing, and a mentor or two put me close to ministers, made me a frequent attender of meetings of Cabinet and its committees, and placed me right at the centre of two transitions of power from one government to another.

Eventually, this cumulative experience was sought out. I have spoken at professional development sessions for political staffers and for public servants, as well as to university classrooms. My tenure as the secretary to Cabinet started memorably during a Cabinet retreat in

Saint Andrews, New Brunswick, when the new prime minister swivelled around and asked whether I had any advice for his new ministers on how to work effectively with the public service.

As a deputy minister, I had already learned that the most important conversation to have with a new minister, fresh from the swearing-in ceremony, was not one about files or events but one about the craft of being an effective minister.

I had a key role at the Privy Council Office in three transitions of power. When power shifted from Jean Chrétien to Paul Martin, it shifted to an experienced minister from the same political clan, which meant that the transition was relatively straightforward compared to the later hand-offs from Martin to Stephen Harper and then from Harper to Justin Trudeau. Both Harper and Trudeau, attending their first Cabinet meeting as the chair, looked across a table dominated by colleagues who were new to being a minister and, in many cases, new to being a Member of Parliament.

In each case, I was one of the leaders of the public service team that met with a team of advisers to the new prime minister – the "transition team." An intense period of decision making accompanied the start-up of the new government. Not many people have taken part in this process three times, and these experiences impressed on me how similar the conversations are with any group new to governing. A friend of mine used to distinguish between the "what" and the "how" of a government – what policies it pursues versus how it conducts itself. This is an attempt to capture a lot of those briefings and conversations about the "how."

New politicians or politicians in new roles get help. The House of Commons runs excellent programs for new members of Parliament and their families. Ministers are welcomed in two ways. Their core department usually prepares a suite of material on their role and authorities, upcoming issues and events, personal safety and cybersecurity, and a sense of the policy landscape that they're about to enter. The caricature of public service briefings is a stack of binders; but these days, the material comes on secure laptops and tablets.

In addition, the "Centre" – the prime minister's political team, or the PMO, and the prime minister's department, or the PCO – prepares orientation sessions and issues ministers a handbook on governance titled *Open and Accountable Government.* This handbook has been updated after each election to better reflect the incoming government and is available on the Internet to all Canadians. The Privy Council Office also focuses on what the new prime minister needs. I fondly remember showing Justin Trudeau around the old Cabinet room in the Centre Block.

All of this material can be a valuable resource, but in my experience, it is a bit too safe, doesn't quite capture why things are the way they are, and doesn't delve into the real tradecraft that determines success. This book is intended as a supplement to those other sources, but I also hope to convey, to anyone who is interested, what ministers and prime ministers are expected to learn on the job, sometimes painfully.

There is a special feeling and swirl of emotions around the start-up of a government. I was at Rideau Hall for the swearing-in ceremony for the Martin, Harper, and Trudeau Cabinets and remember the buzz of anticipation, the pride beaming from family members, and the sense of history. I was at their first Cabinet meetings and recall the palpable sense of optimism and determination to make a difference by finally putting aspirations into action. I recall on another occasion escorting a visibly trembling new minister to the assigned place at the table.

But I was also in the room for the very last Cabinet meetings of the Chrétien, Martin, and Harper governments. The mood was more sombre and reflective – marked by a sense of finality in one respect but also by a feeling of leaving unfinished business behind. There was a streak of joviality and end-of-term camaraderie that had been forged in common experiences. But I remember a senior minister, defeated in the recent campaign, turning back to look one last time at the room with a pained expression. I have sat across from an exhausted minister who was suddenly forced into resignation by events that spiralled beyond recovery.

The chance to sit at that table rarely comes a second time, and once it is over, it is over.

WHO IS THIS BOOK FOR?

It is possible that this volume will be picked up and annotated by some future minister or prime minister. Most politicians I have met are life-long, avid students of history, including accounts of political campaigns as well as political biographies and memoirs, and they can piece together from these works indirect insights into governing. My goal is to be more direct and to make it a bit easier.

My ambition is broader. I want to take anyone who is interested in Canadian politics – those who study it, those who work close to the decision makers, and those who observe them through the lens of media coverage – into the rooms where the discussions take place and where decisions are forged. More than that, by looking beyond the very narrow spotlight on Question Period and beyond the hallway media scrums that show up on the news, I hope to convey the broader scope of what prime ministers and ministers actually do most of the time. These are hard jobs, especially if you want to do them well.

POLITICS VERSUS GOVERNING

The difference between politics and governing is a matter of scope. There are many dimensions to Canadian politics that I will not touch on or that I will touch on only to the extent that they affect the central topic of governing: the exercise of the power to make decisions on our behalf.

My entire career was effectively on the government side of our democracy. My contact with backbench members of Parliament and with the other side of the aisle was limited to appearing at interrogations conducted by parliamentary committees of the House and Senate and at occasional briefings offered to members of Parliament and critics. Someone else will have to write a handbook for being an effective member of the Opposition or an effective backbencher.

Some topics that political scientists like to explore, but that I will not, are relevant to governing because they determine which small set of people will have the opportunity to govern. Take, for example, how political parties choose their leaders and party constitutions, a process that affects internal dynamics and the leader's vulnerability to challenge from within. These internal battles have become a regular feature of governing in Australia but remain rarities in Canada. However, it matters in Canada how parties set the rules to determine which candidates will become members of Parliament and then how safe incumbents will be.

Elections matter. The only people who get to govern, and exercise power, are the ones who win elections. But I have no experience in the business of winning elections and no advice to offer. Clearly, the Canadian electoral system matters a lot. The "first past the post" election system of choosing our members of Parliament has more than one effect on who gets to sit in the Cabinet room. As has been well studied, it tends to distort the geographical mix on the government team, providing the prime minister with a surfeit of choice in some provinces and a dearth in others. It exacerbates tension among regions. But it has also spared Canada, so far, the complications of forming and running multiparty coalition governments, which are commonplace in many other democracies, including the United Kingdom.

That is not to say that governing and politics are separate realms. Politics is always present in the deliberations of the elected, as it should be in a democracy. Governments are supposed to be responsive to electorates. The core agenda of any government, the default setting to which it seeks to return if driven off course by events, is to deliver the things that it promised voters in the last election and to signal the things that it will do more of if re-elected.

So my view is that it is useful to understand how politicians and their political staff think about issues and what factors they are likely to weigh in order to sustain and extend their mandate to govern. I was always annoyed to hear some version of the phrase "they're being so political" spouted as a complaint. Of course, they are. Sometimes, it is important for public servants to weigh in with other considerations of broader public interest, such as sustainability or a longer time horizon, but in the end, it is the elected who are accountable.

The most important trait among ministers seems to be geography; every minister is from somewhere. Much of what happens in the Cabinet room is affected more by regional considerations than by divergence in ideology or by who supported whom in the last leadership contest. I vividly recall sitting in on a meeting of the Trudeau Cabinet as clerk in 2017 and feeling a wave of déjà vu, as the same topic had come up for Brian Mulroney's Cabinet in the 1980s when I was a junior officer at PCO and the same regional tensions were surfacing. If I had closed my eyes, it would have been difficult to tell one meeting from the other.

The art of governing a democracy often lies in finding the right mix of politics and policy. It takes political skill to craft policy initiatives and legislation that will overcome resistance or inertia and gain enough public support that they become immune to reversal. And it takes a record of competent, responsive government to sustain political support.

PEOPLE

Much of the "political science" that is taught is about institutions and processes. Not that there is anything wrong with that. My goal is to convey the importance of the human dimension. I have come to the view that the best preparation for government is not the study of law or economics but the study of psychology.

In the end, a Cabinet or a caucus of members of Parliament is a collection of humans, and they will be strongly affected by human cognitive biases, responses to incentives and disincentives, and the dynamics of group behaviour. I don't think that there is a right set of character traits to be effective in governing. Rather, it helps for leaders to be self-aware and for the people who support them to make adjustments to systems and processes that accommodate or compensate for very different leadership styles and temperaments, different learning styles, and different ways of getting to decisions.

I set out to capture the direct advice that I would give to a new prime minister, a new minister, and a new deputy minister, who will be asked to support a minister. But they form a connected package; understanding what the other is going through may make someone more empathetic and effective in their own role.

I have observed and talked to several prime ministers and dozens of ministers over the past three decades and have worked closely with political staff from both teams who have earned the right to exercise power on our behalf. It is difficult to convey the breadth and variety of the people who make our democracy work. Some start strong and fade. Others grow into the role. Some are better at the job than others. But overwhelmingly, they approach their role with dedication, perseverance, and a sense of greater purpose. Canada will need them if we are going to keep moving forward toward our aspirations and our potential.

2

POWER IN THE CAPITAL

More than once, I addressed a parliamentary committee or briefed a journalist on background and was taken aback when I had to stop and explain some aspect of Canadian governance. These were people who had lived and worked in the nation's capital, both in and around government, and I just assumed that they had internalized most of the basic design principles. Often, people had unconsciously taken on American or British constructs and missed something that is distinctly Canadian. It turns out that a lot of people simply press on with their particular roles and don't have a good line of sight into what others are doing or why. What follows is a quick walk through the essential features that shape how Canada is governed.

LET'S START AT WESTMINSTER

To use a 2020s metaphor, the core DNA of government in Canada is the Westminster model of parliamentary democracy inherited from the United Kingdom and shared with a handful of other democratic countries. There are important "variants" in how this model has evolved, and the context for governing in Canada is unique in many ways.

Federalism

One essential feature of Canada is federalism, a political system where government power and responsibility are divided between a national government and regional governments. There are democratic systems with some aspects of federalism throughout the world, and the models of federalism are not static. Within the small Westminster club of countries, the United Kingdom is not a federation but it has moved to "devolve" some jurisdiction from Parliament in London to legislatures in Scotland and Northern Ireland, and it will continue to grapple with internal dynamics. Ireland is not a federation, but despite its history, retains most of the essential features of the Westminster model. It has spliced in an elected president instead of the British monarch. Some Australians would like to do the same thing.

Canada and Australia grafted the Westminster parliamentary model onto a federation of provinces (states in Australia) and territories. Being a federation means that at times, in discussing issues, we should take a look at Australia but also at Germany, Switzerland, the United States, and other democratic federal systems. There are many times when comparisons to the Nordics, New Zealand, and other small unitary states such as Singapore and Estonia fall apart. There is an entire academic industry built on Canadian intergovernmental relations, which peaked in the national unity and constitutional rounds of the 1980s and 1990s, and Canadians with experience in intergovernmental relations have always been sought out by other countries and international organizations for their advice.

The point is that any Canadian prime minister and most federal ministers will have to learn how to work with the other levels of government in order to achieve their goals. They will also have to navigate the federal state's commitment, made and extended over the past half-century, to working in two official languages: French and English.

The Charter

Arguably, Canada's particular, and most important, modification to the Westminster model was

> " The point is that any Canadian prime minister and most federal ministers will have to learn how to work with the other levels of government in order to achieve their goals. "

to splice the Charter of Rights and Freedoms into our Constitution in 1982. That was when we parted company with Australia. The alteration to the underlying Constitution shifted power away from the legislature and toward the courts and citizens, both individually and in collective groupings such as language minorities and Indigenous peoples. This shift away from the legislature was deliberate, intended to be permanent, and highly controversial at the time. It puts constraints on the options available to Cabinet, constraints that are different from those faced by Cabinet's counterparts in London or Canberra, and it allows court decisions to disrupt and shape the agenda of the government. Canadian governments are often reacting to the courts.

British Stylings
The small cohort of people who govern Canada perform the executive functions of government.

Think of them as the executive branch but with British stylings.

The monarch sits at the top, represented by the governor general. Laws are adopted by Parliament but come into effect through Royal Assent. It is the governor general who summons and dissolves a session of Parliament. The governor general gives legal effect to a host of executive branch decisions by signing an order-in-council – hundreds of them every year. The role of the governor general can become more substantial in the aftermath of a close election if it is not clear who should be invited to form a government.

In the Westminster model, the prime minister and the other ministers are there to advise the monarch – to serve as a private council, or Privy Council. Ministers become ministers by first being sworn in as privy councillors and taking an oath to faithfully serve the monarch before they are sworn in as ministers with specific roles. The prime minister's department is the Privy Council Office, headed by the Clerk of the Privy Council, who is the secretary to Cabinet – literally, the note taker and guardian of all of Cabinet's paperwork.

Essential Ottawa acronyms are "GIC" (governor-in-council), and "OIC" (order-in-council), or the governor general's actions on the advice of either Cabinet or an individual minister. These acronyms are used with reference to an executive decision, an executive order, or an executive appointment.

The stylings and titles in Canada's Parliament are also British, and they are on full display when the governor general arrives to read the Speech from the Throne (i.e., the Speaker, the mace, the Usher of the Black Rod, the fact the House is summoned to the Senate chamber).

The Confidence of the House

The key point about Canada's Westminster model is that the people at the core of the executive branch – Cabinet – are also answerable to Parliament and are part of the legislative branch at the same time. This is where American analogies can lead us astray.

Unlike in France or the United States, there is no direct route to becoming the head of government or the chief executive. To get the chance to form the government, you have to win a sufficient number of seats in Parliament, and to stay in government, you have to do it again within a few years. To be prime minister, you have to be the effective leader of an effective political team from across the country, and you must pay attention to the political prospects of all its members as you govern.

Unlike in the United States, to become a Cabinet minister and secure one of those scarce seats at the Cabinet table, you have to win a plurality of votes in some part of the country, and to stay in Cabinet, you have to keep winning. To get into Cabinet, you must first convince about 25,000 fellow Canadians that you should be their Member of Parliament. Some promising ministerial careers have been cut short, or in a few cases, never launched, because local voters withheld or withdrew their mandate.

Yes, there is a back door. In the past, some prime ministers have appointed a senator to Cabinet or have named someone as a minister before that person has secured a seat in the House of Commons. But these cases are the rare exceptions that reveal the convention: prime ministers and ministers come from the elected members of Parliament.

New party leaders with aspirations to the top job know that they will have to get into the House as soon as possible, and more than a few

> "
> Any prime minister knows from the painful experience of predecessors not to take local electors for granted and is highly unlikely to name a star candidate as a minister before that person's election has been secured.
> "

have used by-elections as their admission ticket. Any prime minister knows from the painful experience of predecessors not to take local electors for granted and is highly unlikely to name a star candidate as a minister before that person's election has been secured.

Confidence

The strong convention that prime ministers and ministers come from the cohort of members of Parliament also reveals another core principle of the Canadian Westminster model: the answerability of the executive to the legislature. There isn't a "separation of powers."

The government can obtain and hold office and exercise its executive functions only as long as it demonstrates that it has the "confidence" of the House of Commons. Its powers are largely created and constrained by legislation. It can spend funds or raise taxes only with Parliament's approval. This isn't a small point; England had a civil war and executed a king to establish the principle.

So a lot of the art of governing in Canada is about the executive successfully navigating the dynamics with Parliament. Some of the challenge is about how to engage with the Opposition, especially during periods of minority government. Since 2016, a new dynamic has arisen in dealing with a Senate largely composed of independent members. But much of the challenge is also about interactions with the government-side caucus of elected members of Parliament.

Prime ministers also have to work with the team that they have – the one that voters pick for them – and they spend a lot of time and energy shoring up weaknesses, building up its strengths, or finding new team members.

Continuity, Coverage, and Restraint

For the purposes of performing executive functions, there is unbroken continuity. A minister is the minister until the next one is sworn in. If someone quits or is incapacitated, someone else automatically takes that person's place as an acting minister, who is chosen from a list approved and issued earlier, usually when the first Cabinet is sworn in. The list of acting ministers is kept continuously up to date.

There is also complete coverage of answerability to Parliament. Every federal entity, ranging from big departments to small agencies and independent tribunals, has a minister. When setting up a government, moving ministers around, or creating new entities, people at the Privy Council Office check to make sure that everything is covered.

Ministers do not have the same number of entities to answer for. They have a portfolio that the prime minister assigns to them. Some may have responsibility for a topic or theme with very little administrative support from the public service. Others may have a dozen or more entities ranging from big departments to small agencies. Regardless of the number of entities, most ministers exercise a large suite of powers and assume accountabilities created by laws passed by Parliament. Some of these laws are generic and apply to all ministers, such as the 1985 Financial Administration Act and the 2006 Federal Accountability Act. Other accountabilities are specific to a portfolio and may be set out in legislation in some detail.

Strictly speaking, ministers can exercise these powers at any time, but the core convention of Westminster is that they should be answerable to Parliament and should act with the confidence of the House. So during those times when Parliament isn't in session because an election is under way, another convention kicks in: the convention of restraint.

During an election campaign and until the next Parliament starts up, there is a period when the executive has all of its powers but agrees to exercise them "with restraint," acting essentially as a "caretaker." No two elections occur in the same context, so different issues that may need interpretation arise each time, but the basic principles are clear. To head off disputes about interpretation of the convention, the prime minister provided explicit instructions first in 2015

The public service is emphatically part and parcel of the executive.

and again in 2019 at the start of the election period with the publication of *Guidelines on the Conduct of Ministers, Ministers of State, Exempt Staff and Public Servants during an Election*.

Nonpartisanship and Delegation in the Public Service

Fairly regularly, one reads about the public service in language implying that it is an independent branch of government. It is not. The public service is emphatically part and parcel of the executive. Public servants work hard to deliver the policies and programs determined by ministers and are responsive to the agenda of the elected government. They also report to Parliament on what they have done with funds and authorities, and a dozen or so agents or officers of Parliament are constantly looking over their shoulder. The 300-plus federal entities exercise powers and authorities conferred on them by Parliament, and for every single one of them, there is a minister who is answerable to Parliament.

The misunderstanding probably stems from two aspects of modern public administration: nonpartisanship and delegation. Over the course of the past century, there has been sustained effort to take political partisanship out of public service staffing and the awarding of contracts, and to remove it from many categories of appointments.

The other aspect is that distance has deliberately been created between ministers and the public service entities that they answer for – and real fences exist. Some powers and accountabilities have been formally assigned to the deputy minister or the equivalent top civil servant, who may in turn delegate them further down the chain of command. In other cases, such as regulatory functions or spending programs, the minister formally has final approval but delegates decision making to officials. This arrangement serves the purpose of efficiency and practicality but also builds public confidence that the services and transactional outputs of government are not driven by partisan considerations.

This distance between ministers and the public service creates two issues. One is that it creates lots of potential for a minister to get into trouble by straying across lines. The other is that the role of senior public servants is not well understood. They have been chided for being too obedient and compliant in their service to ministers but also caricatured as puppet masters calling the shots behind the scenes. Neither is a true reflection of the nuanced relationship.

WHO HAS POWER AND WHAT IS IT GOOD FOR?

Concentration at the Centre?

Observers of Canadian governance often focus on the concentration of power around the prime minister.

One line of argument centres on the scope for a prime minister to dominate politics and decision making. This argument suggests that a prime minister in command of a solid parliamentary majority can drive government in a quasi-authoritarian way. There is some truth to this view, especially when comparisons are made to the American president, who always has to struggle with Congress and work within a fairly well-defined box of executive powers. Canadian prime ministers can usually be confident of getting approval of legislation, spending, taxes, and programs, and they can be reasonably certain that their actions will stick until an election and a change of government. A prime minister with a parliamentary majority can get a lot done and change the trajectory of the country.

More importantly as regards governance, prime ministers get to pick a lot of the other actors in the constellation of governing. They recommend the choice of governor general, senators, the senior judiciary, the governor of the Bank of Canada, the head of the military, and the head of the national police. They choose, shuffle, and fire Cabinet ministers and appoint senior public servants and the heads of hundreds of federal entities. In the hands of a domineering personality, there appear to be no "checks and balances" and no "separation of powers."

This situation has led to a lot of scrutiny and analysis of the prime minister, almost to the exclusion of looking at anyone else, and it has focused the attention of journalists and lobbyists on who may have proximity to or influence on the prime minister.

The reality is more nuanced. Others, such as Ian Brodie in his 2018 book *At the Centre of Government: The Prime Minister and the Limits on Political Power,* have explored this issue in greater depth. Two points are worth making here.

First, over the years, a lot of practices and conventions have built up that constrain the prime minister's discretion, that make arbitrary decisions less likely, or that hold the prime minister accountable. Much of the discussion about Stephen Harper toward the end and about Justin Trudeau during the pandemic years was focused on whether these mechanisms were being eroded.

> " One of the permanent questions
> in Canadian governance is the
> nature of prime ministerial
> power and where it fits in. "

Second, in practice, prime ministers have to constantly work hard to achieve the alignment and momentum that are needed to get things done. They have to attend to their ministerial team and their caucus. They have to anticipate and respond to the views of the Senate. They need to engage with premiers and Indigenous leaders. They must be mindful of what the courts may have to say. They have to contend with inertia and with resistance to change, both inside and outside of government.

One of the permanent questions in Canadian governance is the nature of prime ministerial power and where it fits in.

Are Ministers and Members of Parliament Nobodies?

With all the focus on the prime minister, some commentators have cast aspersions on the ministers and members of Parliament, who are essential to moving the government's program forward through Cabinet and Parliament. Some have disparagingly compared them to sheep.

The analogy is not a good one. Yes, the basic Westminster software says that members of Parliament and ministers cannot behave like American members of Congress and senators. Their mandate comes not just from their constituency but also from the shared mandate of the team. The government can retain the confidence of the House only if its members stick together. If it loses something considered a "confidence vote," then it is game over for all of them. Government members of Parliament will ultimately have to go along with the group when they are told to do so by the government whip, or they will have to leave the team.

Similarly, there is a strong convention of Cabinet solidarity. Once the ministers have decided on a course of action, they all defend and advocate for that decision, whatever their private views or misgivings. Ministers tasked with advancing a bill or a program do their best to be successful. If they feel strongly enough that they cannot support what the team has decided to do, they are expected to leave Cabinet.

So ministers and government-side members of Parliament have to exert their influence on decisions *before* the government team locks in, and on important matters, they have to do so behind closed doors. In exchange, they are given considerable latitude to speak their mind at meetings of Cabinet or meetings of the

> " One of the most important arts of governing in Canada is the successful management of the dynamics and personalities within Cabinet and the government caucus. "

government caucus. The confidentiality of these discussions is key to making it all work; without Cabinet confidence, it isn't Cabinet government. Without a safe space for candour, behaviours would change, and the power dynamics would change.

It is probably because the deliberations of Cabinet and the caucus are private that some people erroneously assume that they don't matter. They do. One of the most important arts of governing in Canada is the successful management of the dynamics and personalities within Cabinet and the government caucus. This task can become more challenging the longer a government has been in office.

The "Centre" of Power

Each minister is supported by a political office led by a chief of staff and a senior official, usually the deputy minister of the largest entity in one's portfolio. These people are key to any minister's success. They operate in a world of constant dual accountability.

On the one hand, they are answerable to "the "Centre," with political staff responsible to the PMO and deputy ministers responsible to the PCO. They know that they can be moved on or out if they aren't seen as performing, so they show the centre considerable deference. Furthermore, they spend a lot of time and energy participating in the mechanisms set up by the PMO and the PCO to coordinate work across the government. It can look a lot like central control.

However, these mechanisms also provide effective ministers and their teams with a way to persuade the "Centre" to pursue a course of action. Furthermore, the chief of staff and the deputy minister are also directly accountable to the minister, and the key is that they have every incentive to help the minister to succeed. One of the ways that the PMO and the PCO assess them is by how well their minister is doing. These two people spend a lot of time and energy directly with the minister (and each other) trying to solve the myriad tactical issues that arise, and over time they can form strong professional and personal bonds.

It isn't quite symmetric. Deputy ministers and their officials have their own set of defined accountabilities and obligations to be transparent, whereas political staff have up to now largely been shielded by an "invisibility cloak" from these laws and practices. You generally will not see the traces of their activity in Access to Information disclosures or in appearances at parliamentary committees. Political staff have less job security and retirement income; they are in precarious employment.

What Is It All For?

The route to governing is through elections.

This statement reveals one of the key dynamics of democratic politics: governing and winning elections drive each other. The two cannot be completely separated. Many aspects of governing are inherently and legitimately political acts in a democracy.

There are some areas where it is best to keep partisan politics out of public administration. It has taken a century of work, dozens of laws, the creation of institutional watchdogs, and constant vigilance to take partisanship out of civil service staffing, the awarding of contracts, and most appointments.

Many aspects of governing are inherently and legitimately political acts in a democracy.

But taking out partisanship isn't the same thing as taking out politics. A democratically elected government is always mindful of its electoral prospects and shapes policies and decisions to enhance them, or at least not to damage them. It works hard to deliver its own election platform and can do so with the legitimacy of an electoral mandate. It tends to make choices that please its allies and confound its opponents.

Media coverage of daily politics often starts and stops here. A typical "analysis" is whether this or that action or event makes the re-election of the government more likely or less likely. Are the polls responding favourably or unfavourably?

But for every government that I have worked with, it has never been only about winning elections or following what polls and focus groups are saying. What is the point of doing all the hard work of winning an election and getting into government if not to be in a position to make decisions, to make choices, and to set the country's direction? Sometimes, the point of winning elections is to be able to govern, not the other way around.

All those people out there in stakeholder groups, or writing columns and op-ed pieces, or participating in consultations are trying to nudge and influence decisions. Most of the people in Opposition dearly want to have their turn in government or miss the days when they used to be there. There is an old Ottawa saying that the worst day in government is better than the best day in Opposition. That is debatable and some days clearly untrue, but it goes to the point that governing has a bigger purpose than winning the next election.

At some basic level, the best way to win elections is to be seen as a competent and trust-worthy group of people with the right skills and values to govern. The best way to lose future elections is either to mishandle issues that go to ethics or basic competence or to run out of vision and ideas regarding where to go next.

For prime ministers, governing and electoral prospects are interwoven. Prime ministers who want to spend years governing and making a difference need to retain the support of their members of Parliament and help both incumbents and potential candidates to win their seats next time. If leaders start to look to them like they have exceeded their "best before" date, have become a liability, or are less appealing to voters than someone else in the party, they will soon be in trouble.

Political Capital

The other place where governing is inherently political is in the use of "political capital." Political capital is said to be a stock that changes

over time through trust, goodwill, and interactions and relationships between politicians
and electors.

A stock of capital isn't a perfect metaphor for
the phenomenon, which is more mysterious
and elusive. Political capital has within it meas-
urable elements of standing in the polls and
approval ratings, and there are software models
that regularly estimate the probability of winning the next election. But it also has elements
of brand and reputation. It is associated with
empathy and "getting it." Deeper down, there is
an underlying element of trust and confidence,
and even deeper, there is an element of legitimacy and the consent of the governed.

Think of political capital as a resource used
in governing. As a starting point, we can say
that governments with lots of political capital
get more done. Some people think of it as finite
and believe that it will inevitably be dissipated
over time – either mindfully or passively. Over
time governments make more and more decisions that may disappoint or irritate clusters of
voters. Political capital can be spent fighting
battles worth having but it can be depleted by
issues that go to ethics or competence. I once
heard issues of arrogance and entitlement
described as the "kryptonite" of governing.
Eventually, a prime minister can simply reach a
point of overexposure where a lot of the public

are tired, making a prime minister vulnerable to their desire for something fresh and new.

Governing well and getting things done can slow the rate of dissipation and perhaps even restore the stock of political capital for a time. Taking actions and making decisions can build or restore reputation and trust. New decisions can help to dull the memories of past errors or troubles. Indeed, some actions come along that can be both high-risk and high-reward. Governments are often remembered years later for their bolder moves, both the ones that worked and the ones that didn't. This is the juncture where governing crosses into making history.

3

ADVICE TO
A PRIME MINISTER

If you become prime minister, you must have done something right. Otherwise, why did your party pick you to lead them? Why did more Canadians vote for your party than the others? You have now joined an exclusive club with a small membership, and there aren't many people around who have been part of it.

You are eager to plunge in and get going. You have a good sense of *what* you want to do. You should still pause and reflect on *how* you want to be prime minister. One way to start is by asking how the job came to you. There are two core scenarios:

1. *You won the leadership in Opposition and then won an election, probably after stints as a Member of Parliament and as the leader of the Opposition but perhaps not.*

You're starting the mandate of a fresh new government.

This would be Stephen Harper, Justin Trudeau, Brian Mulroney, Joe Clark, and John Diefenbaker, whose first Cabinet meetings were ones they chaired as prime minister. If this is you, you have a lot to learn about managing Cabinet and the caucus.

2. *You won the leadership while your party was in government, and sooner or later you will have to secure your own electoral mandate. You probably had some time as a minister, either very recently or perhaps before you took a break from politics. You showed your stuff enough that your colleagues came to see you as plausible in the big chair – and you had a chance to see governing up close and to observe your predecessor.*

   This would be Louis St. Laurent, Lester Pearson, Jean Chrétien, John Turner, Kim Campbell, and Paul Martin, all of whom had time to observe predecessors up close. You can focus on your own approach to the job and on your new role of pulling it all together.

Next, check the tank for political capital:

How strong is your mandate from your party and within your parliamentary caucus?

> *Do you need to trigger an election soon in order to refresh the team and bring in new talent, or is there time and a sufficient plurality that you can use by-elections?*

> *Are your rivals for the leadership likely to come on board and cooperate?*

> *Does your predecessor as party leader cast a big shadow?*

> *Are you in good shape in the polls and fund-raising relative to your political opponents, or will they be smelling blood and coming in for the kill?*

Whatever the political scenario, you want to get off to a good start. It is possible to make up for a fumbled start-up but not easy.

THE PRIME MINISTER'S ROLE

Hats, Hats, and More Hats

When you become prime minister, you immediately take on a daunting array of roles:

Member of Parliament for your constituency

Leader of your political party

Head of government for Canada, responsible for dealing with the leaders of other countries and international organizations

First minister in the federation, responsible for dealing with thirteen premiers

Minister for your own department (or PCO) and political staff (or PMO)

Chair of Cabinet – the first among ministers

Leader of your parliamentary caucus

Each of these roles is supported by a distinct system and by a team with specialized knowledge and skills. In any given week, one or two may dominate your attention and your schedule, but most likely you will have to deal with some aspect of each. Being prime minister is all about continuous multitasking, which won't stop until you leave the job.

Together, these seven roles will require more time than you actually have, so be mindful that management of your schedule is a key to making progress.

> Being prime minister is all about continuous multitasking, which won't stop until you leave the job.

Time for family, for exercise or relaxation, and for old friends outside of politics will be squeezed to the margins unless you work to protect it. By now, you have figured out what seems to work for you – your own approach to exercise or relaxation and to work. Do you prefer to finish up as much as you can at the office, or do you like to take work home?

Try to consciously create a structure and a routine that work for your family so that you can return to that routine any time you are knocked off stride. It isn't easy to fit spouses, children, and parents into the grind of your new job. Work will tend to crowd out time for things that you used to do, like watching sports, binge-watching television series, or staying current on pop culture. Reading anything other than work-related documents will soon start to feel like a luxury. If your past pursuits are important to you, you will have to force time for them into your schedule.

The Masks under the Hats
You will present several personas to people around you.

The public will see the one on the news. That mask is a mosaic picture built from short clips and sound bites.

Journalists and stakeholders will accumulate longer-exposure pictures of you through their interactions or by attending events.

Your Cabinet and the caucus will see the persona you present at closed-door gatherings filled with people from your political tribe.

A small number of advisers and public servants will see your approach to the myriad briefings and meetings conducted away from the cameras.

Your political staff have helped you to cultivate your political persona and will continue to do so. Their strategies must have worked for you in the leadership race or election that brought you the job of prime minister. However, on the day that you become prime minister, your persona immediately changes. You take on the attributes of the office and incumbency. Your

> ... people may not remember what you said, but they will remember how you made them feel.

freshness starts to wear off, scars accumulate, but at the same time, your gravitas can increase. Your every move, gesture, and word will be scrutinized for content and tone by people with strong confirmation bias to see what they want to see. This confirmation bias grows stronger the longer you are in office.

Behind closed doors, you should still be mindful of the persona that you present. As the saying goes, people may not remember what you said, but they will remember how you made them feel. You have a big impact on their motivation to work hard and well. At times, you may have to keep your own fatigue and irritability in check. That doesn't mean having to spend a lot of time in small talk or to hide your emotions. Economical use of feedback goes a long way. A word or two of thanks for work well done or a quick aside to congratulate someone or to acknowledge any personal issues is all that you need to offer. Encourage your chief of staff and the clerk to slip you prompts.

You should not hold back negative feedback. If you think that the analysis was thin, the arguments weak, or the options lacking in imagination, say so. How else will it get better? The ideal tone is candour delivered with civility. People who deal with you will be strongly impacted by small moments of good humour or snippy outbursts of bad temper. Your staff can keep an eye on whether individuals are feeling

> **"** The ideal tone is candour delivered with civility. People who deal with you will be strongly impacted by small moments of good humour or snippy outbursts of bad temper. **"**

bruised or demoralized – some people are more needy or resilient than others – and can remind you to correct for it later.

Meetings should be inclusive but should last only as long as needed, not expand to fill a time slot. If you can end a meeting early and gain a sliver of time, get up and leave. Don't worry; you will never run out of things to do. Back at your desk, there will always be documents to read or sign and calls to place.

Set Your Own Tone and Style

Political staff will urge you to seek as much distance as possible from your predecessor and to put your distinct stamp on governing. They may do this because they think that you have lots of political capital or because they are desperate to acquire some. Your sense of urgency will depend on whether the next election is four years away or more imminent.

Putting your own mark on governing will of course be much easier if you have just toppled the other team rather than having taken over the leadership of a party already in power. If you are taking over the party and the government from your predecessor, it is a real challenge to find the sweet spot where the public will keep in mind the good parts of your predecessor's and your party's brand but will see you as fresh. More likely, you will be tied to the parts of your predecessor's legacy that the Opposition and the media will gleefully point out. Many prime ministers didn't last long after taking over a party from a long-serving predecessor.

If you have come into power from the Opposition, the contrast with the predecessor you have just defeated will give you an assist for a few months, but within a year, given the relentless focus on you as the prime minister of the day, collective memory will fade, and you will fully own your own brand and track record.

Your political staff will innately want to make a fast start. After the leadership race or the election campaign, they will be pumped with adrenalin and a sense of having been proven right, and they will be confident in their skills; you won, didn't you? They will sense that the clock is already running and will feel that they need to get things done, especially while the other side is demoralized from a loss and

> " Use the start-up period to
> pick a few things that will test
> your team and enable you to
> score some early wins. "

probably in some disarray. They will be excited
by their new roles and eager to try them out.
The default is impatience.

The trick is not to overdo it. Use the start-up
period to pick a few things that will test your
team and enable you to score some early wins.
If you have toppled the other side, then getting
started with a few reversals can signal not just
that the government is "under new management" but also that there will be a change in
tone and style. You will want to take early actions
that send a positive message to the voters and
allies who supported you and pinned their
aspirations on you. Most likely, the campaign
that has just ended will give you a menu to
choose from: "If elected I will ..." Pick a couple
of undertakings that will prove your mettle.

Jean Chrétien cancelled the procurement of
helicopters and reversed the Campbell government's move to privatize Toronto's airports. Paul
Martin cancelled the nascent political history
museum and abolished a government communications agency. Stephen Harper moved

quickly to walk away from the Kelowna Accord and to put in place a different version of child care support. Justin Trudeau's first decision was to reinstate the long-form census, and he moved quickly with a tax cut for the middle class.

Announcing a general freeze on hiring or spending right away will cause more problems than it is worth. If you want to tap the fiscal brakes, wait a few weeks and get your minister of finance and your president of the Treasury Board involved and answerable.

You will want to make changes among some of the leadership positions across the dozens of government agencies. It isn't easy to fire people, but you can move people out as long as you are ready to defend the severance and exit packages. The law has established rules of thumb for compensation, and usually some sort of settlement can be reached. A few people, notably the officers of Parliament, are appointed "at good behaviour," and it is all but impossible to remove them. You are stuck with them until their term runs out.

This is an area where you will need to tread carefully. Firing someone carries the risk of causing aggrievement, and with a lot of time to lash back, the person may feel justified in leaking and may cultivate the media and the Opposition. Be sure that the consequences are worth it.

> " Firing someone carries the risk of causing aggrievement, and with a lot of time to lash back ... "

Pundits like to talk up the first "100 Days of Decision" and will set up an early milestone to pass judgment on the government. Ignore them. These early days won't affect the next election very much, unless it is imminent, especially if you stumble later. Voters tend to think in terms of "what have you done for me lately?" and they will recall only a few signature initiatives. Those actions are just as likely to come in the middle or latter parts of your mandate – as it takes time to develop and deploy matters of real substance.

What you can do in the early days is imprint a tone and style and start to establish a reputation for competence, and it doesn't take many actions to do that.

Give yourself some time to put together a decent Speech from the Throne.

Think through whether you will publish ministers' mandate letters and what should go

*in them because you will immediately start
being marked on them.*

*Have your first four of five government bills
identified as opening moves to keep the
House of Commons and the Senate busy.*

Start work right away on the first budget.

*Use your first couple of international trips to
get familiar with that side of the job and to
test your international affairs team.*

One or two big things is enough to get going,
unless you have inherited a specific crisis to
manage or a Dumpster fire to put out.

The second half of your first year, after the
opening moves have been played, memories of
your predecessor have faded, and the Opposition has started to regather strength, is the
crucial time to build momentum and your list
of accomplishments.

Your Clerk and Chief of Staff

You will sit at the apex of a number of support
systems and distinct streams of information
and advice, and no one else will have the same
perspective as you. Out of necessity, many of
the people around you will be specialized and
only partially or vaguely aware of what other
colleagues are up to. You will soon start to see
linkages and trade-offs as well as risks and

opportunities that others may not. Your ability to do so will grow over time.

The longer you are in office, the more you will have accumulated the story behind any issue: How did we get here? What was tried in the past? How did it play out then? Was I involved in a Question Period scrap? The upside of this accumulation is that you can quickly get to discussing a new way to address the issue. The downside is that you may be unconsciously reluctant to look at it differently.

A handful of people will come close to seeing the whole picture and have the greatest ability to anticipate your interests and perspective. The clerk runs your department, the Privy Council Office, and is at the apex of public service support. Your chief of staff runs your political team, the Prime Minister's Office, and is at the apex of political support. Together, they can influence the timing and quality of the information and advice that you receive. They will have the broadest perspective and will most likely bring a depth of experience.

You will instinctively want one or both of them at meetings because it makes sense to get their input right away so that your directions and the necessary follow-up tasks can be efficiently put into action. Both the clerk and the chief of staff chair regular gatherings of the senior people in their respective networks.

> " Over the long haul, you will want to widen the inner circle. "

They are like two parallel nervous systems for you and your government.

But there is a trap to avoid. You can end up pinning these two people down and overcrowding their schedules, reducing their flexibility to do their jobs. If you make them the only people who brief you, they will have to spend many hours reading and getting briefed themselves, and you can create a potential bottleneck as well as distortion in the signal. Over the long haul, you will want to widen the inner circle. Allow other people to come and brief you or to sit in on your meetings and phone calls, and let the clerk or chief of staff catch up later.

Most prime ministers will try to have a regular time slot with just the clerk and the chief of staff. You will have to pick a frequency and a venue that work for you. Most likely, they will also meet regularly without you in the room to debug issues or to sort out the essentials that you need to know or hear before you make a decision.

There is a risk of becoming too dependent on these two, and sometimes they will need to be somewhere else or will need to take a break. It would be in your interest to have a second person to turn to on each side – a deputy clerk in the PCO and a principal secretary in the PMO. No two cases or constellations have been the same for your predecessors, so you will have to sort out this matter early.

You should also take their pulse every few months on personnel issues. Who do they see as performing well or struggling among the ministers, the chiefs of staff, and the deputy ministers? You should undertake this task in a more rigorous and structured way once a year but check in informally from time to time. Everyone you see will be putting on a game face and trying to impress you. No one will want to bother you with personal struggles or health and family issues. You can develop blind spots about people.

HEADS OF STATE AND POLITICAL LEADERS

The Crown

As prime minister, you are the head of government, but the head of state in Canada is effectively the governor general, who exercises a role and powers on behalf of the monarch.

There are a few ways that you will interact with the governor general ("the GG") and the monarch that flow from the institutional arrangements in Canada's Westminster system and its membership in the Commonwealth. You will need the governor general to invite you to form a government and to preside over the swearing-in of yourself and Cabinet. You will have to ask the GG to deliver the Speech from the Throne to open the new session of Parliament. After these early interactions, your need for personal contact with the GG will drop off in frequency.

There is a reasonable chance that at some point during your mandate, you will get to pick the next governor general, perhaps more than once if you last long enough. Actually, you will be submitting a recommendation to the monarch. You will personally win or lose some political points as prime minister based on how your pick performs as governor general during a term of somewhere around five years.

The first instinct of many prime ministers' teams is to focus on the symbolism and signalling that the selection creates. There is a custom of alternating among English and French speakers and expecting a high degree of bilingualism. Gender, race, ethnicity, geography, and profession all may be factors to consider.

It isn't an easy personnel matter. Not everyone who fits your optimal profile will want the job, and some of the people who lobby for the job will not be the ones you want to pick.

> " Not everyone who fits your optimal profile will want the job, and some of the people who lobby for the job will not be the ones you want to pick. "

Give some thought to readiness and suitability to perform a unique job. It is a very isolated and sometimes lonely position, and the GG will be the target of a lot of sniping and grumbling. Spending by the governor general has long been a fetish of some journalists and news outlets. The job requires personal resilience. It is a job that involves a lot of travel and outreach and meeting many people, both in Canada and in other countries.

Three groups of Canadians who take their long-standing relationship with the Crown very seriously and who will expect a lot of access and contact with the GG are the military, veterans, and Indigenous peoples, especially First Nations who have signed treaties. You will want to pick someone who will be relatable to these groups and play a role in their events, commemorations, and celebrations but also be able to stay out of current politics related to defence, veterans, or Indigenous policy.

The GG will play a role in key moments of the life cycle of your government, starting with the formation of a Cabinet after an election or leadership change and ending with its dissolution. Most of the time, these are ceremonial matters, and the governor general will routinely assent to legislation and sign off on the executive orders that you recommend – including the orders to summon, prorogue, or dissolve Parliament or to call a general election or a by-election. Occasionally, there may be some controversy and discussion among "experts" about whether the GG can or should exercise independent judgment and reject your recommendation. You will get your advice from the Clerk of the Privy Council and from the Department of Justice. The GG will get advice from legal counsel. Rideau Hall usually maintains a roster of distinguished scholars and retired judges to draw upon.

The ceremonies related to opening Parliament, reading the Speech from the Throne, and swearing in Cabinets or individual ministers can be useful reminders of the gravitas of being the government as much as opportunities to reinforce the brand and message of the day. The governor general can also be a useful diplomatic asset – deployed to host visitors or to travel to other countries as part of an outreach effort.

Your interactions with the actual monarchy will be infrequent. Visits to Canada by senior members of the royal family are planned and handled by a combination of the pertinent teams in the United Kingdom, staff at Rideau Hall, and specialists at Canadian Heritage, and you may be asked to play a role in welcoming them, accompanying them, or hosting events, but you can arrange to share the load with the governor general and some of your ministers.

If your work takes you through the United Kingdom, you may be asked to pay a call on the monarch if you haven't crossed paths for a while. Every two years or so, you will be expected to attend a gathering of leaders of the Commonwealth and will have some interaction with the sovereign or a representative. You may also find yourself together with members of the royal family at commemorations of the two world wars.

It is up to you whether you want to have more regular contact with the governor general. You both occupy unique roles and may enjoy comparing notes, and you may see each other as allies and confidants or not. Your families may get along or not. Whether you get along personally doesn't ultimately matter. Some prime ministers developed a practice of regular monthly lunches with the GG, whereas others went long stretches with little contact, leaving it to the Clerk of the Privy Council to maintain regular contact and to keep the GG up to date.

Heads of Governments and Organizations

Some of your time will be taken up by phone and video calls and meetings with the heads of government of other countries and with the heads of international organizations.

Much of your interaction with the leaders of other countries or international organizations is done effectively through phone and video conversations. It is relatively easy to secure half an hour or an hour in their calendar, and you will want to accommodate them in yours.

Most prime ministers (and their counterparts) routinely reveal that an international call took place and provide some sort of summary of what the subject was and any outcomes – a "readout."

There will be times when you might prefer to discretely call without making it known, but they will be rare, and doing so puts you at risk of becoming hostage to someone from the other government who may be inclined to leak that the call took place, which people are known to do.

If the meeting is face-to-face, there is often a period of post-meeting "media availability," followed by the posting of photos to social media.

Phone Calls. Although you can just say, "Get me President/Prime Minister X on the line," in practice these encounters are rarely spontaneous. The following situations are typical reasons to arrange a call:

Prep calls to iron out "announceables" just before you visit another country or its leader comes to Canada.

Prep calls before an international gathering to align positions on issues. Canada is a member of a lot of clubs, which means that you will be on the receiving end of a lot of calls. Every few years, Canada hosts a summit, and you will have extra duty trying to pull leaders toward some degree of consensus on the "summit outcomes."

Calls to lobby the other leader to support a Canadian candidate for a leadership position in an international body or to support the selection of Canada for membership in a particular body.

"Closing" calls to resolve a negotiating impasse. Prime ministers rarely get involved until the late stages. Nor should they. You will want to stay out for as long as possible, or over time it will disempower your ministers, and issues will start coming directly to you.

You will be supported by a team of international relations specialists in both the PCO and your political office. Each side should have a lead foreign policy adviser. These specialists will work out with you a format for notes, talking points, and "cheat sheets" to make the best use of the calls and meetings. It may take a few times to get it the way you want it, so don't hesitate to ask for changes. Most often, a quick preparatory briefing will suffice to remind you of the purpose and your objectives. Every contact, no matter how brief, should be purposeful.

You may want to be joined for a call or meeting by your lead minister – trade, foreign affairs, finance, and so on – but many times it isn't necessary for you or the best use of the minister's time. Similarly, you may want to be joined by the ambassador to that country or by your "sherpa" to a summit, at least for any pre-briefing. Whether or not you actually want the safety net of someone who knows the files and the backstory, bringing such people in can help them to do their job by conveying to the other side that they "have the ear" of the prime minister. It can also improve the timeliness and accuracy of follow-up.

One complication is that you have to assume that attempts are being made to intercept and overhear all of your communications. This is one of the world's other oldest professions. Your whereabouts are easy to track, and you are easy to target. That is why you will have access to secure meeting rooms and secure phones and video conferencing. You will be frustrated by the times when the connection is difficult to

> **"** ... you have to assume that attempts are being made to intercept and overhear all of your communications. **"**

establish or the call drops, but the extra protection is important, so don't cut corners.

Face-to-Face Meetings. You are much more likely to meet the leaders of other countries face-to-face around the margins of broader gatherings or events that you both are attending than through a deliberate bilateral visit. Each leader has calendar pressures. Each will make a different valuation of the utility of visiting Canada or receiving you abroad. Foreign leaders are more likely to come to Canada if they are on the way to or from somewhere else, perhaps New York or Washington, or if they have a significant diaspora in Canada, or if they have specific trade promotion goals.

It is more likely that you will end up at the same place for a "summit." Canada is a member of many clubs, large and small: the G7 and G20, the Commonwealth, the Organisation internationale de la Francophonie, the Asia-Pacific Economic Cooperation, and the Organization of American States are just some of them. This membership means that you will always have an ample array of potential "pull aside" meetings to choose from. Leaders find themselves together at commemorations of significant events. There will also be the inaugurations and funerals of other leaders, but generally you can hand these representational visits over to your foreign minister, the governor general, or a former prime minister.

You can try to proactively manage your foreign engagements by asking for an update in writing once or twice a year from your foreign policy team that lays out options for outgoing and incoming visits and seeks your approval. Don't be passive and let them pile up as non-decisions, or options will foreclose and fewer "deliverables" can be prepared. You should also ask for a briefing before each summit that includes your options for side meetings. However, you will find yourself making last-minute adjustments.

The White House
Many of your international relationships can be important at times, but the most important one will always be with the president of the United States. There are many other players in the American political constellation, and it is worth investing in a broad and deep outreach. Choose an ambassador to Washington whom you trust and who will listen and be attuned to

> " You will personally be
> assessed by Canadians on
> your skill in handling the
> dynamic with the president ... "

you. You may want a formal or informal team of ministers and senior officials permanently tasked with the multifaceted US relationship. You can enlist premiers, federal Opposition leaders, and your predecessors to help out, and you will find them generally willing to do so.

You will personally be assessed by Canadians on your skill in handling the dynamic with the president, especially if the political alignment is not evident (think Pierre Trudeau and Richard Nixon, Stephen Harper and Barack Obama, or Justin Trudeau and Donald Trump). You get the president that the American voters give you, and regardless of political stripe, you have to do everything that you can to open and maintain a constructive relationship.

It may be important to your own agenda to build a positive agenda of initiatives related to trade, security, and infrastructure. At a minimum, you may have to work hard to vaccinate against the risk that the Americans will take Canada for granted, forget about the impact on Canada of actions aimed at other countries, and side-swipe us unintentionally. Look for opportunities to be helpful to the American president on something important to the United States or to the president personally.

Working with the Premiers

Many of the issues that you face will bring you into contact with the leaders of the provincial and territorial governments. They may be directly involved in delivery and implementation of initiatives that your government wants to advance, or they may be delivering policies and programs that complement or run counter to yours. They consider themselves the spokespersons for their part of the country, with some cause. Your counterparts in the United Kingdom and New Zealand don't have this complication to grapple with.

The relationship that you will have with any given premier will be only loosely related to political party. You may be able to get along with and do business with someone from the other stripe, just as you may find someone from your stripe to be a thorn in your side. The relations that the premiers will have with your federal ministers from the same part of the country will range from very close to very strained depending on past history, especially if your ministers have spent some time in provincial politics. They may or may not like or get along with the federal party leaders with whom they

> " The most productive way to work with premiers over time is one-on-one and away from cameras. "

share a party label. Even if a provincial government is more or less aligned with yours, a certain amount of friction about who announces and takes credit for things is inevitable.

The most productive way to work with premiers over time is one-on-one and away from cameras. Phone calls and short meetings can get a lot sorted out. This work can lead to announcements and public events that you both can benefit from.

Do I Have to Meet Them as a Group? You will run into the temptation to convene a meeting of first ministers from time to time. First Ministers' Meetings can be used to reassure Canadians that their federation is working or to elevate some issue to a higher plane of national importance. You may want to use them to secure an agreement that aligns the effort of all the governments and reinforces a sense of national common purpose.

However, as prime minister, it is rarely to your advantage to get together with the premiers as a group. Yes, something may come up on your watch – a major international negotiation or an emergency – and keeping premiers in the loop will be of mutual benefit. You may want to meet from time to time simply to project to the public that you are collaborative or to deny the more difficult premiers and pundits an easy line of criticism that you are arrogant and disrespectful. But don't expect too much of substance to come from these meetings and don't let expectations build if you do decide to convene one.

The numbers and the incentives at a gathering of all the premiers are not in your favour. There are thirteen of them, and the arithmetic is that it only takes a few of them to block progress, to water down initiatives, or to make your task more difficult. Generally, they will come to agreement only on a lowest common denominator. That usually means what they think you should be doing for them.

In any given year, a few of the thirteen will be getting close to their election, a time when their incentive is usually to be critical of the federal government, at least in public. Some of them will bash you in the media and then call you and try to make up, saying some version of "it's just politics."

Premiers have their own incentives. They don't want you to be fettering their discretion, especially on the issues where they run the delivery systems: health care, social services, education, and local infrastructure. They have a very strong incentive to get you to transfer federal funds to them so that they don't have to raise provincial taxes or borrow on provincial credit.

So the predictable outcome of any gathering of premiers is going to be a call for you to increase federal transfers with as few strings attached as possible. They will assign their best people to put pressure on you in the buildup and even during the meeting. Premiers have gone back to this playbook every year for decades.

Supporting You in Managing the Federation. You will find that the federation works just fine without your personal involvement or a lot of meetings of first ministers. Every year, there are many gatherings of federal, provincial, and territorial (FPT) ministers and senior officials who work together or share emerging knowledge and practices. They come up with ways to align

> " You will find that the federation works just fine without your personal involvement or a lot of meetings of first ministers. "

efforts. Some are pan-Canadian, some regional, and some bilateral. You have a group of specialists in your Intergovernmental Affairs Office, and they can keep an eye on the FPT world for you.

You will have to determine the mandate and bargaining room of federal ministers and officials on the bigger issues in play with the provinces and territories. It can be a lighter or heavier touch. You should require your ministers to come to one of the Cabinet committee meetings before major FPT meetings in order to ensure that their approach aligns with that of their colleagues.

If you do end up meeting all of the first ministers together, an easy way to show progress at the subsequent media scrums is to task one or more of these ministerial tables to work on an issue, with as focused a mandate as possible, and then to report back to the first ministers with findings or recommendations.

You may or may not want to name a minister of intergovernmental affairs. It can be a useful slot to help balance out your Cabinet or to solve a personnel issue. You don't really need one, as the heavy lifting of FPT files will be done by ministers with line responsibilities: finance, infrastructure, environment, health, and so on. Premiers want a direct relationship with you. So unless you have one or two clear tasks in mind and won't have to do a lot of supervising, you are probably best to pass.

> " The key point is that the arithmetic of the Canadian federation works against the federal prime minister. A handful of premiers is enough to delay or block. "

The key point is that the arithmetic of the Canadian federation works against the federal prime minister. A handful of premiers is enough to delay or block. There will be ebbs and flows in the tone and climate of intergovernmental relations. So when windows of alignment open up and progress looks possible, press hard and don't waste them.

Indigenous Peoples

Every Canadian prime minister of the past half-century has spent significant time, energy, and political capital on "Indigenous issues." It would fill a different book to cover the evolution of the legal, political, and economic context and the ebb and flow of the attempts at constitutional amendment, structural change through legislation, and political accords. Since the entrenchment of Aboriginal and treaty rights in the Constitution in 1982, the courts have generated

> As prime minister, you will have to decide how to structure your own engagement with Indigenous issues and your relationships with Indigenous leaders.

a stream of rulings and new jurisprudence that have affected not just what the federal government does but also how it does it. The doctrines of the duty to consult and the honour of the Crown constrain the executive branch of government. Not only do Indigenous issues encompass specific relationships like the Indian Act, treaties with the Inuit, or legislation targeting child and family services, but there will also be an Indigenous dimension to almost every issue that the government will address.

As prime minister, you will have to decide how to structure your own engagement with Indigenous issues and your relationships with Indigenous leaders. There are many precedents to draw from, but you will have to find your own way. You may want to create a special Cabinet committee or coordinating group and a supporting secretariat in the Privy Council Office. You may want to lean heavily on a particular minister, but you will find that several of them will be heavily involved. Your choices for minister of justice and minister of finance will make a big difference in this area. You may want to create structured, predictable engagement meetings with the main representative political organizations, separately or together. That will help you to sort out priorities into a work plan, create deadlines, and give direction to ministers, officials, and the staff of Indigenous organizations.

You will have to decide how to factor Indigenous leaders into the machinery of intergovernmental relations. Should they be invited to all meetings of first ministers or for parts of them, and, if so, which ones? Do you want to attempt an event with high risk and high reward such as a First Ministers' Meeting devoted to Indigenous issues or a version of the Crown–First Nations Gathering of January 2012? You will have to decide to what extent the protocols of Indigenous gatherings should infuse your own government, starting with the very first swearing-in ceremony.

You will discover that Indigenous leaders, no matter how critical they may be of you and your government in public, will seek to establish a good working relationship with you personally and can be candid and constructive in private. They face their own challenges with their executive bodies and memberships. Make time for private meetings and calls. But be careful that you don't end up undermining your ministers by incenting people to go over their heads and directly to you.

MANDATE AND APPOINTMENTS

Mapping Your Mandate

Early on, you should ask your political staff and the public service to take a stab at mapping out their best approximation of the full mandate. If you have a majority, you should be able to deploy four budgets and eight sessions of Parliament – two fall and two winter-spring. There will be obvious big events that you can plug into that map, such as hosting or attending international summits and major commemorations.

PCO staff will be delighted to draw up the dense business lists that your government will have to contend with. They will probably have done so while you were off winning the campaign or the leadership race. Here are some "known knowns":

Sunsetters: *Many laws were passed with a clause triggering their complete sunsetting or a mandatory review by Parliament. Past budgets approved some spending initiatives for a fixed period, usually a few years, and on your watch, you will have to decide to continue, cut, or augment.*

Court Cases: *The trajectory of controversy-filled court cases up through the appeal courts and toward the Supreme Court can be forecast, at least the probable timelines.*

Elections: *Provincial and territorial elections can be anticipated to a large extent now that fixed elections are common, so the chances of important shifts in the constellation of first ministers can be anticipated.*

No work plan or agenda will survive contact with realities, and there will be major shocks and surprises to come. But there will be value in reducing the numbers of true surprises and in having a compass to steer by. While you are personally dealing with any crisis, other parts of your team and the public service can be working to keep initiatives moving forward until you are ready to focus on them.

> No work plan or agenda will survive contact with realities, and there will be major shocks and surprises to come.

You don't have to get everything done in your first year – but you don't want to waste it. Indeed, there is a widely held view that the second year of the mandate is the hardest one. Most likely, the Opposition will have sorted out any leadership issues and identified its most skilful attack-minded players, and your own team will have discovered just how grinding their new lives can be. Some will have stumbled by then on performance or behaviour or both. Your ability to say "it wasn't us" will end by the time of the second budget and the second round of reports from the wide array of oversight watchdogs.

Make sure that you set up some way to check in from time to time on how your mandate is progressing. You can get an array of tools from both the PCO and the PMO sides of your team, and you can make good use of periodically convening retreats for the caucus and Cabinet.

Executive Branch Appointments

As the prime minster, you have the final say on GIC (or executive branch) appointments before they go to the governor general, who signs the orders that give them legal effect.

Decide early how best to deal with appointments – a process that should be in place before they end up in your signature book. Typically, appointments come in as recommendations from a minister who is answerable for an entity. Many will go to Cabinet for vetting. Usually, the appointment will be announced by the minister, but you will want to be aware of proposed appointments in order to ensure that you are satisfied with the overall flow and stock.

Strictly speaking, you can usually appoint just about anyone you want, unless one of the statutes spells out specific requirements, but it is in your interest to have a process that screens and culls candidates for security clearances, potential conflicts of interest, degree of bilingualism, and basic competency. Bad appointments will lead to headaches down the road, and you can be sure that someone out there – media, stakeholders, or the Opposition – will be conducting in-depth social media research every single time to see if the appointment can be criticized.

The prime minister is responsible for appointing the following:

Ministers and parliamentary secretaries. *You don't just name these people but also define their role and title.*

Senators. *It is your call, but you decide what process to use to identify candidates. In the past, prime ministers asked their staff to generate regional lists of potential senators. More recently, a process of open applications and regional selection committees has been used. You can create your own process.*

Officers of Parliament. *As of 2021, there are nine officers who help Parliament to exercise its oversight role, including high-profile ones like the auditor general and the privacy commissioner. They work for Parliament, but you get to appoint them. The Canadian compromise that prevents you from appointing tame watchdogs and that holds you to account is the requirement for consultation with the leader of the Opposition and with the leaders of the other parties. So far, Canada has not seen as much partisanship as the United States. These appointments are usually for long tenures and are strongly protected from termination. Over time, the output of those you appoint will affect how your government is perceived, so it worth taking the time to get these appointments right.*

Deputy ministers, associate deputy ministers, and a basket of equivalent senior public service positions that head up federal institutions. *These appointments come in as recommendations from the Clerk of the Privy Council, and you will be asked to approve the person, the job classification, and perhaps some aspect of compensation. Sometimes, there will be just one or two recommendations, and sometimes the list will be longer, indicating a "shuffle."*

Key actors in the executive functions of gov-
    ernment, such as the chief of defence staff,
    the RCMP commissioner, and the governor
    of the Bank of Canada. *These appointments*
    typically follow the recommendation of a
    specific minister.

A Deputy Prime Minister?

You don't need to name a deputy prime minister (DPM) for the purposes of day-to-day governing. It may be proposed to you as a way to
solve a personnel issue posed by one of the
party elders or defeated leadership candidates
or as a way to make a gesture to one of the fac-
tions within your political party.

The bigger decision is whether to formally
    You can somewhat lighten your own work-
load by having a DPM chair specific committees
or short-term task teams, take the heat in Question Period from time to time, or clear the under-
brush of small issues. It isn't a lot of extra work
for the Privy Council Office to support a DPM
unless that person is also the minister for something else, like finance or foreign affairs, which
creates a lot of minor day-to-day challenges
sorting out scheduling and flow of documents.

The bigger decision is whether to formally
carve out and delegate a precise range of your
decision-making territory or to use a DPM as a
generic second-in-command with responsibilities that shift from week to week and month
to month.

> " ... you should not appoint a
> DPM early in your mandate. "

In the end, a DPM is not going to be much of a political shield. You cannot escape the visibility and accountability for everything that your government does. You are the primary target.

There is an internal risk that, as the DPM and especially the DPM's political staff become a distinct node in the network of influencers, friction will build up with your own team or with those of other ministers. Once you name someone as the DPM, you will have disappointed half a dozen other ministers. Ottawa gossip will frequently turn to the prospects of your DPM as a future leadership contender, which can be an unwelcome distraction. Once a significant number of people are musing about a life without you as prime minister, your own power will start to ebb.

On balance, unless you have a specific political signal to send or a tricky personnel issue to solve, you should not appoint a DPM early in your mandate. Wait until you have gained a few years of experience, know your own preferences better, know your top performers, and can make the choice and define the role with some confidence.

CABINET

The Cabinet-Making Puzzle

If you are wise, you haven't made a lot of promises to put individuals in Cabinet or, even worse, to give them specific jobs. Sometimes, doing so is a necessary part of convincing someone to run for a seat or to stay in politics, but there are at least two good reasons to refrain. First, promises reduce your flexibility – your degrees of freedom – to solve the Cabinet-making puzzle. Second, they diminish a key source of your power; you want the members of your caucus and Cabinet to see you as the final arbiter who can advance or sideline political careers. You want them to worry and in some cases to fear you.

Putting a Cabinet together is an iterative process. You will start with one list and then go back over it looking for matches and balance, move a few pieces, and then do it again and again.

Start with geography. *The election outcome will give you the pieces to work with; unless you win a huge majority, you are likely to have an abundance in some regions and a shortage in others. Someone who represents a lonely outpost of your party pretty much goes right into the mix, and you can fuss*

> **"** You want them to worry and in some cases to fear you. **"**

over which portfolio. For other regions, you will have more choices but will have to disappoint more people and find other tasks for them.

Then fill a handful of key assignments – the core of the team. *Some jobs are more important than others. They may be the ones that are generally seen as "senior" and immediately bestow status and standing in exclusive international clubs – finance and foreign affairs, for instance. These ministries are often a good place to put a former leader or someone you bested in the leadership race, as it bonds them to your success, at least for a while.*

Now, match people to the three or four issues central to the agenda that you have just laid out for Canadians. *You want your best players in these roles. Ignore the conventional wisdoms about the pecking order and focus instead on what projects are too important to fail.*

At first, some of your team may have a bit of a head start because they have served in a federal or provincial Cabinet before. They can be a good fit for the portfolios that bring more risk of bad things popping up, as they are less likely to be easily flustered or paralyzed. They also tend to make good committee chairs, which will be important for keeping your government moving forward. One needs a particular background to be the minister of justice or the attorney general, but there are always lots of lawyers to choose from. You will need someone who can drive your particular agenda in law reform, who cares about the administrative side of the justice system, and who can be trusted to make good choices in appointing judges and dealing with the prosecutorial service.

Finally, round out the slate, keeping in mind the overall balance and the picture that you want your team to represent. *Looking at the team, you should weigh the representation of gender, race, and ethnicity as a factor; you are going to be judged on it. Sometimes, prior professional and life experience makes for a good fit with a particular role, but it can also be a trap, as the minister may turn out to be too rigid in looking at problems and solutions or too unwilling to rock the boat with the professional community that the minister knows and may intend to return to someday.*

It does matter who gets to sit at the Cabinet table – to be part of the thirty or so. Fewer than one in a million Canadians will be ministers. They all matter. Not only do they take the lead on their own portfolio, but they also get to offer views on everyone else's files. They can nudge the outcome, adding ambition and momentum or resistance and caution. They can help the team to hone messages and to deal with the caucus.

The diversity of voices and the representativeness of the group sitting around the table will make a difference to the tone and content of deliberations. Arguably, these factors can improve the quality of decisions by reducing the chance of having blind spots and adding to the range of inputs.

Think of Cabinet as a portfolio of assets – some more valuable than others. The good news is that if you run into performance issues, you can make changes or divest.

Setting the Structure of Government

One of the core prerogatives of the prime minister, another wellspring of your power, is making the final decisions on how the executive branch of government is structured and what decision-making process it uses. This is the "machinery of government." Often, what you will be deciding is what the government will present to Parliament in the form of a bill.

Because the subsequent parliamentary process often leads to amendments, the people in charge of the legislative agenda will come back to you if necessary and ask if you want to agree to the amendments or want to go back and try to reverse some of them.

During the transition period between the election and the swearing-in of your Cabinet, one of the first orders of business is to set the structure of Cabinet and its committees. While you were busy winning the election, your transition team may have already engaged you to get some direction. You may have some prior experience to influence your views.

In many ways, it is an exercise in flow hydraulics. How will issues, proposals, and options move through the government to become actionable and implementable decisions? Where are the filters, the valves, the potential bottlenecks where pressure and temperature will increase?

In other ways, it is an exercise in time management. Time for Cabinet to get together is a precious resource. In any given year, once you lop off weeks when the House is in recess, you might squeeze in about thirty meetings of between two and four hours. Let's say 100 hours. Committees can add another quantum of time, perhaps another 100 to 200 hours, that can be used to dig deeper into bigger issues and to clear out the minor transactions.

You can choose to have an inner group that you chair and to convene full Cabinet less frequently, often styled as a Priorities Committee or an Agenda Committee, or you can use full Cabinet as the main deliberative group. You can set up a range of committees focused on thematic areas such as foreign policy, economic policy, or Indigenous issues and on functions such as parliamentary affairs, communications, or managing emergencies. You will need both. You may want to personally chair certain tables, such as security and intelligence.

There is no right answer between a small number of larger and broader committees and a large number of smaller and more focused committees. They will tend to add up to the same thing in terms of total time used each year. Recent improvements in secure meeting technology have made it easier for ministers to participate in meetings while away from downtown Ottawa, so they can literally cover more ground than they used to, and it is easier to convene them in groups.

You will want to keep in mind that there is always a scarcity of really gifted chairs, but picking chairs is a bit like picking Cabinet since people will scrutinize your choices for gender and geographic balance. The extra status and workload are things that you can use to reward allies, to keep rivals busy, or to develop a

> " There is no right answer between a small number of larger and broader committees and a large number of smaller and more focused committees. "

deeper bench. Effective chairs help to keep your government moving forward, provide solid due diligence on both policy and politics, and sustain team morale.

You will be asked to sign off on the membership of the Cabinet committees. Some slots will flow naturally from the portfolio assignments, but you will want to round out the lists with other ministers in order to broaden the range of perspectives, help with their development, and balance out region, gender, and other factors.

You will have to keep an eye on workload. There is a tendency to unconsciously go back to the same ministers who are proven workhorses and put them on four, five, or six committees, especially at the beginning of a mandate. You risk wearing them out or trapping them out of sight in Ottawa. Taking a longer view, you will want to give newer ministers a chance to grow and become ready to take on more. So don't miss the chance to shuffle chairs and Cabinet committee assignments from time to time, even if people are staying in the same portfolio jobs.

Ministerial Roles

You decide what bundle of assignments to give each minister and what title each should use. It doesn't have to be the one set in a law or the names of departments. You have a lot of design options. You can use the language of a title or the choice of bundles to signal policy or political intent. You can make one minister responsible for more than one thing and put together combinations.

You can assign a minister a role that is more general – seniors, rural development, youth, digital government – but if you do, make sure that it is clear from the outset which deputy minister and which public service units will provide support. The clerk will work through these matching issues with you and propose moving public service units around if necessary. Who will be the main political adviser? Your chief of staff will have ideas.

You will have a Cabinet of around thirty ministers, who will be answerable for around 300 entities. Sometimes, a statute spells out explicitly which minister goes with an entity, but increasingly the practice has been to leave the language in the statute at "the minister," which gives you more flexibility to move ministers around. A wonderful tool called the Transfer of Duties Act makes it easy to move around accountabilities without immediately having to go to Parliament and reopen a bundle of statutes. You can clean up the legislation later, although doing so will require the sort of dense administrative bill that often lingers on the Order Paper and dies at the end of a session.

One of the core exercises in the transition period will be to run through every entity in order to make sure that there is a minister for each one – and that every minister's bundle of accountabilities is clear, makes sense at the time, and can be posted for all to see.

You can make changes to the design of departments, agencies, boards, and tribunals – pulling them apart to create new things or merging them together. You can expand or shrink the mandate of existing entities, adding to or subtracting from their powers and obligations. There are several reasons why you could want to do this:

- *the need to "fix things" after a failure or breakdown seen as a crisis*
- *the emergence of new issues that now need greater attention*
- *shifts in policy direction or new views on how to deliver old functions*

- *pressure from stakeholders or recommendations from parliamentary committees*
- *the need to fulfill an election promise to make a specific machinery change*

Changes to the machinery of government often come up as a by-product of a big expenditure review. These exercises generate lots of ideas about increasing efficiency or saving money by terminating something or merging it with something that looks similar. Broader spending reviews make it easier to face down the resistance to doing so, especially if more than one organization is being affected at the same time. So machinery changes have often come in clumps and clusters rather than one-offs.

There can be a temptation to reach for machinery change in order to respond to issues. It makes you look active and in charge and shows that you are breaking with the past. These can be valid goals, but machinery change is a tool that you should use sparingly, with care, and to achieve a clear purpose. It can be very disruptive, burn up valuable time and energy, and cause a loss of momentum and focus. Resistance is inevitable. The effects on the surrounding ecosystem of stakeholders can be considerable. Changes to regulatory bodies have particularly big ripple effects.

> " ... machinery change is a tool that you should use sparingly, with care, and to achieve a clear purpose. "

Machinery changes can often outlast you or your government. Ask yourself and grill your advisers about what political purpose, what policy purpose, and what administrative purpose this proposed change will serve. Why do you think that this change will achieve that purpose?

You will have alternatives to changing the formal structures. You can use special purpose task teams that come together and are wound down. As long as the task is clear and one person feels accountable for getting it done, they tend to work well. They don't succeed when accountability is diffuse and the task fuzzy. You can always lock in these combinations as enduring machinery changes later if they have proven their value.

Chairing Cabinet Effectively

Cabinet time is a precious commodity. With only about 100 hours a year to allocate, it is an art to get the most out of the time that Cabinet will have together. When it comes to Cabinet business, you'll be asked to

Approve the agendas for upcoming Cabinet meetings and any Cabinet committees that you personally chair; it's your job to deem that something is ready for discussion and, if it goes well at the meeting, ready for decision.

Arbitrate and approve any loose ends or details regarding what Cabinet decided at an earlier meeting so that an initiative can proceed to announcement and implementation.

As the chair, you will want to spend some time reading the material in advance and will want to allocate a sliver of time right before the meeting to go over the expected choreography, desired outcomes, and any late-breaking developments that may affect the meeting. You may need to allocate another sliver of time right after the meeting to download any pressing follow-ups to your immediate team – after which you will be dragged off to prepare for the afternoon Question Period. While you were in the Cabinet meeting, the Opposition had all morning to prepare their attacks of the day.

Cabinet business will typically be taken up with one or two major items per meeting, plus up to a dozen smaller transactional items, including appointments. Cabinet is the governor-in-council approving a GIC appointment. The one or two major items will generate wide interest because they can affect the whole team's success and reputation. The other transactional items will emerge from the committees and be of greatest interest to the sponsoring minister and some subset of the table.

The PCO will ask you the week before to approve the agenda so that it can be circulated with the related Cabinet papers several days in advance. One of the constant quirks of ministers' behaviour is that, despite being quick to complain that they are not getting Cabinet papers soon enough, they tend to fuss over and put off signing and sending in their own proposals until the last possible hour. Both this regular interaction with the PCO and related discussions with your senior political advisers give you an opportunity to elevate some items to the main agenda or to push off other items for more work before they come to the table. If you do that too often, you are going to build up a snowbank of unprocessed items, so sometimes the best call is to bring an item forward for a first kick, see what the issues are and where your ministers are lining up, and then ask for it to be brought back again. It's your Cabinet, and you should not hesitate to intervene in the pace of its deliberations. PCO staff

> " It's your Cabinet, and you should
> not hesitate to intervene in
> the pace of its deliberations. "

will always map out two or three meetings in advance, be ready to give you their take on the agenda, and make adjustments as they go.

Don't hesitate to change the sequence of items on the agenda for a particular meeting in order to ensure that you give the most important items enough time. You can do so at the last minute. Yes, the agenda was circulated in advance, but the Privy Council Office will have brought all the necessary people over and will keep them in a holding room off to the side of the Cabinet suite, where they will be ready to be ushered in or on standby to go online.

Trust your instincts about how to chair Cabinet meetings, which will get even better over time.

Faced with the constraints of time, prime ministers have taken very different approaches to the transactional items and appointments. Some have tried to gain time and shorten discussion by setting as a default that items on the annex of committee recommendations will be deemed approved unless someone speaks up. Others have taken the time to read out each item and open it up for questions and comments.

When the list of proposed appointments comes up at Cabinet meetings, most prime ministers have allowed anyone at the table to request that one be set aside and brought back later. It has been very rare to discuss the individuals. Ministers tend to be vigilant about the composition of the stock and flow of appointments in order to ensure that there are enough from their part of the country, or from gender groups, or from other demographics. In every Cabinet, one or two ministers keep a close eye on bilingualism. The PCO will help you to keep track of these patterns, and you may want to share report cards with Cabinet from time to time. There are about 1,500 positions, and only a few hundred come up for renewal each year, so it will take time to dramatically shift the composition of the overall stock of appointees.

Not all Cabinet discussion is about making decisions. Sometimes, you will want to use a Cabinet meeting just to give the team an update on how something is progressing; ministers are less prone to be caught out if they have a common information base and understand what the common messaging is supposed to be. Here, items of importance will tend to flow from events – international summits, provincial elections, First Ministers' Meetings, military deployments, disasters – and they could displace time from the pre-planned agenda. Sometimes, ministers just need to talk about the politics of the day and will ask that the room be cleared of everyone except the clerk and the senior staff from the PMO.

What you will notice is how little time is available. You will need to be mindful of the clock during meetings. Going around the table and taking a couple of minutes of comment from each minister would burn an hour. Some are more concise than others. Some read talking points provided by their department. Some want to relitigate a discussion at committee. Some have talking points that some stakeholder or lobbyist has managed to slip to their political staff. Prime ministers have tried different techniques to ensure that there is a bit more time for discussion, such as limiting the number of slides in a presentation, banning presentations altogether, or putting a clock in front of them that flashes a light after a time limit on interventions has expired. Your tone and demeanour may encourage or discourage chattiness and rambling. It is going to be a fine line. If you are too brusque, you can sap the morale of ministers trying to do their best. They will start to question why they are working so hard and giving up so much if they aren't being listened to. Your position as leader will be strengthened if the team feels included and heard.

Owing to the reality of limited time, it is going to be rare to tackle more than two big issues per meeting, and allocating Cabinet time over a whole season is going to be a constant challenge that will leave you feeling somewhat dissatisfied, and many meetings will feel a bit rushed.

But then there will be those meetings when the prep work has been done well and the group comes together to thrash out politics and policy in a lively debate that sets the course for an ambitious move that changes the direction of the country. Those are the moments that can feel electric and make all the drudgework worthwhile.

Cabinet Meetings and the Dynamics of the Group

One of the fundamental principles of Westminster government is that ministers should be free and unfettered to speak their mind at Cabinet meetings and then should close ranks and stand behind the decisions of the team. Cabinet secrecy ensures that they shouldn't have to worry about their views or dissent turning up in the media. They will be slow to build up grudges against colleagues. It is a very different dynamic from that of a municipal council. It is for a similar reason that parliamentary committees move into closed sessions away from the cameras when they really need to get something done as a group.

> "
>
> Cabinet secrecy ensures that they shouldn't have to worry about their views or dissent turning up in the media. "

To make this principle of Cabinet solidarity work, you will have to let people have their say and, perhaps more importantly, make them feel that they have had a hearing or that their views matter to you. Human nature being what it is, some alpha personalities will tend to dominate discussion, so you will want to keep a watchful eye on the others and reach out, asking them what they think, or go around the table so that no one is missed.

As a general practice, prime ministers avoid taking votes at Cabinet meetings. Occasionally, it can speed things up to simply ask for a show of hands, especially when there are fairly clear options in front of the group. But there are good reasons not to do so very often. Making clear who is winning and losing more frequently can feed disgruntlement. Over time, it is a practice that can reveal camps and blocs forming, like on a city council, and allow them to start congealing and solidifying. As the prime minister, you will want to discourage that from happening. You will want ministers to at least try to assess each item separately. You will want the rest of the caucus to see Cabinet as a team and not to be tempted to try to play ministers off against each other.

It is particularly dangerous to cohesion if you know that the issue is going to split on geographic fault lines and that you could be put in the position of taking sides. You will want to cultivate the perception that you are above regional factionalism and have the ability to bring the team together.

You will want to protect your authority as the one who calls the final decision. You may have to make a call that disappoints or frustrates a significant number of the ministers. You may even have to overrule most of them. It is one of the wellsprings of your power to be the one who calls what the "sense of the table" was. You will want to be much more than the chair who keeps a speakers' list and tots up the tally. You are the first among ministers – the "prime."

It is a good practice to avoid the temptation to reveal your views or preferences among options too early in the meeting and before the decision point arrives. For one thing, even if you have a preference, the discussion inside the Cabinet room will allow you to stress test a proposal before you roll it out to a far less friendly audience. A robust and authentic discussion can help you to refine content, marketing, and political tactics. One of the reasons to have Cabinet committees is to make sure that basic due diligence and stress testing can occur without taking up your time. With that done, you can have some confidence in the proposals, and Cabinet can zero in on what is most important.

If you don't develop a good poker face, you will find most ministers reluctant to challenge you. Some of them will rush to align with you whatever their actual views or misgivings. Both effects will diminish the usefulness of the discussion, so hold back.

Cabinet meetings are a very efficient way to dispense positive feedback and to do so not just on the proposals in front of you that week. A bit of staff work can equip you with prompts to acknowledge personal milestones and to express gratitude. Telling ministers that they have done things well or letting them know that you have shown an interest will rekindle their energy and enthusiasm and their appreciation of you as their leader. Whether it was how they handled an announcement or a parliamentary spat, defused a potential crisis, or deflected incoming attacks, the minister will be pleased just that you know about it. Finding a way to work in a thank you to the political staff and public servants behind the minister will have a huge impact on them if they are in the room.

You can also use Cabinet meetings to create a sense of exclusivity and fellowship among the

> " You can also use Cabinet meetings to create a sense of exclusivity and fellowship among the team by sharing stories to which others wouldn't have access. "

team by sharing stories to which others wouldn't have access. Other than at Cabinet meetings, most ministers will see you only in Question Period, or with the caucus, or in news clips about an event. You should occasionally share an anecdote from a recent foreign trip or from a meeting or call that you had. One prime minister would occasionally tell a story to see how long it would take to appear in the media – stress testing Cabinet secrecy.

Cabinet Shuffles

The Cabinet that you start with will not be the one with which you finish the mandate. A bit like with any team, you will want to ensure that new talent is continuously being identified and groomed. Assignments as parliamentary secretaries or as chairs of parliamentary committees or of caucus task teams on specific issues can serve several purposes. They allow individuals to hone their skills and grow in confidence. They add spokespeople to the bench whose strength can be deployed, perhaps to counterbalance a minister's weaknesses in one of the official languages.

These roles also keep people busy so that they aren't sitting around nursing a sense of grievance that they haven't yet made it to Cabinet or have been dropped from it. The only thing more dangerous to your leadership than a frustrated would-be minister is an ex-minister who has nothing to lose and who sees a way back if only you were gone. This is one reason why prime ministers are reluctant to drop or demote someone. The other reason is the need to keep someone in Cabinet from a particular area of the country, which sometimes explains why that person got there in the first instance.

Some of your promising draft picks won't work out, and some late bloomers will emerge. People will leave for any number of reasons. You will want a deep bench. Your political team should be scanning for new talent who could be persuaded to join you mid or late mandate by running in a by-election, but you will want to set a very humble tone and to be very careful how the seat is vacated, as electors have often rejected these selections. Usually, it is better to wait for the next general election to change up the roster substantially. On occasion, if someone just isn't a good fit, it is your job to move that person. They may do better in a different role. Not only do you get better performance by dealing with problems, but it also sends a message to the other ministers to stay on their toes.

PRIME MINISTER'S MEETINGS

Sometimes, the shortest route to a decision is not to meet with Cabinet but to convene the core group of ministers, political staff, and senior public servants and to thrash it out. The outcome may be agreement on what should then be put formally to Cabinet by one of the ministers or at least agreement on where more work is needed and by when. If you do this too often, you risk undermining the solidarity of Cabinet by making other ministers feel excluded or taken for granted. But it can be a useful technique to move issues along, especially if you know that there are strong differences among ministers to be ironed out.

> " Sometimes, the shortest route to a decision is not to meet with Cabinet but to convene the core group of ministers, political staff, and senior public servants and to thrash it out. "

You will want to set up a series of meetings with the minister of finance in the run-up to the annual budget so that you are as aligned as possible on the basic architecture – fiscal targets, themes, signature initiatives. Most prime ministers have retained a "double key" on budget measures that they use discretely so as not to undermine the authority of the minister of finance with other colleagues. The Privy Council Office will have a small team that works on budgets, liaising constantly with the Department of Finance and your political office. In the end, the budget will be recorded formally as a decision of Cabinet. If you find that you need to overrule the minister of finance, do it as privately as possible.

Some prime ministers have attempted to personally keep an eye on the traction of the government toward implementing its agenda. One technique is to convene Cabinet in a retreat-style meeting, usually away from Ottawa. Cabinet retreats are especially useful a few weeks before the House of Commons starts a new session in September or late January. Another is to chair a meeting with a small group of ministers, usually the ones valued for their political acuity, a few times a year to discuss the state of the agenda. Finally, you can ask for a series of "take stock" meetings to check in on a particular area or topic. They can be very galvanizing for the ministers and officials invited.

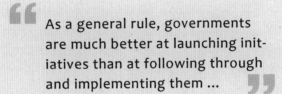

As a general rule, governments are much better at launching initiatives than at following through and implementing them ...

As a general rule, governments are much better at launching initiatives than at following through and implementing them, so you should discuss with your chief of staff and the clerk what sort of feedback loop would work best for you.

EVERYDAY DECISIONS AWAY FROM CABINET

The Paper Chase
A lot of the actual work of the prime minister is done away from the cameras and the spotlight. It is about going to meetings and reading and signing documents. Images from British television of an endless flow of red briefcases – dispatch boxes – aren't far from the mark. One recent prime minister agreed to cap the flow at eighty notes per week. Another agreed to bundle smaller information updates into a weekly package. Another pressed the PCO to get the essentials of any note down to a one-page

summary box. It was the intelligence briefers who first became skilled at the use of photos, maps, charts, and infographics to convey information, after years of writing long, dense texts. Make your preferences clear, and revisit them at least once a year.

Your roles mean that there is a constant flow of information to take in and decisions to be made, some big but many small. The flow won't stop until you leave office. Some of your feedback and direction can be conveyed verbally, but the currency of governing is signatures or initials, and your signature matters the most.

There are two basic types of notes that you will receive. One is limited to conveying information to you, and the other is used to seek a decision.

You will be tempted to do a lot of business through oral discussion at meetings. There are reasons why getting things in writing is often in your interest. One is that your reaction or decision can be garbled, ambiguous, or misunderstood when received by others. People tend to hear what they want to hear or expect to hear. There is far less room for that if you have a document that lays out what you are agreeing to. Implementation will be smoother. Notes can be a touchstone later when people may be arguing about what was decided. They can always come back with new information or new advice.

Getting analysis of options and advice on upcoming decisions sent to you in writing forces others to clarify the course of action and to perform some sort of due diligence before putting it to you. This will tend to reduce the mushiness and will provide at least some analysis of costs, benefits, and risks. It can also turn out to be useful later when reconstructing previous considerations that went into a decision or, if the issue returns in a new form, as it often does, when asked, "What did you know and when did you know it?"

Responding to notes or asking for one is a very effective way to exert direction. Sometimes, you can annotate a clarifying comment or instruction. Sometimes, all you have do is annotate a question, which will trigger a flurry of work to get the answer for you. Sometimes, a simple set of initials will move things along.

You will find people invoking your name, passing on that "the prime minister wants this" or "the prime minister would never agree to this." It is a way for them to exert influence and power, consciously or unconsciously. You will not always be aligned with these intermediaries. You do not want them to become filters creating a comfortable bubble around you or getting you into trouble that you will be answerable for.

You can be direct and clear. Notes to you and your responses will be kept by the Privy Council Office and won't be shared with others.

The PCO will also keep your records away from your successors.

You will find yourself using notes and meetings in tandem and in either order. You may respond to a note by asking for a meeting rather than triggering a lengthy back-and-forth. The flow may go the other way. You may prefer to use a meeting to brainstorm and kick around an issue and then ask for a note to pull it all together and make it coherent and actionable.

Meetings and notes, notes and meetings. They will stop only when you stop being prime minister.

In a typical week, you will be asked to sign the following:

VIP correspondence selected from all those people who have written to you. Your office will have skimmed off and arranged signature books with replies to the foreign leaders, premiers, members of Parliament, and any other categories that you choose to sign personally, with an option to add a personal touch. The rest will be machine signed. You cannot possibly see everything that comes in as routine correspondence, but some prime ministers like to see a sample batch from time to time.

Photos, books, posters, thank-you cards, birthday greetings, condolence notes, and other

> *mementoes that your office will distribute*
> *to continuously cultivate good relations*
> *and to motivate the people working on your*
> *behalf. Don't neglect these items or under-*
> *estimate the impact of receiving something*
> *from the prime minister.*

Signing these types of materials isn't so different from what is required of a minister. But you are the prime minister, and you will be sought out.

The Arithmetic of Encouraging Candour

It will be a constant challenge to create an environment where the people who are on your side tell you what they really think. (This is not a problem for the Opposition or the pundits.) Consciously or unconsciously, people are going to be reluctant to stake out a position that contradicts yours or what they expect yours to be. The power equation is simply unbalanced, and they will worry about whether you think well of them.

Rulers always attract courtiers, eager to agree with you, watching to see what your view might be so that they can serve it up to you as their advice. They fall silent and let someone else be the bearer of bad or unpleasant news. The longer you are in power, the more courtiers you will attract. As a general rule, the more people in the room, the less the probability of candour.

There are several techniques to counter this problem. The starting point is to make sure that the small number of people closest to you feel empowered to challenge you and each other in private without damaging relationships. Prime ministers often encourage candour among colleagues at the first Cabinet meeting after the swearing-in, and you should too. But realize that they will only maintain their candour if they see over time that you mean it, especially that there aren't consequences or reprisals for taking contrary positions.

Another tactic is to agree before a meeting on a good cop–bad cop routine where someone else will be designated to ask the tough questions or argue an alternative, leaving you to hold back until you have seen how the dynamics unfold and the arguments have been stress tested. This role may fit naturally with someone's personality and style, but try to mix it up.

Chances are that there is someone on your team whose history with you from life before politics, time in Opposition, or the leadership race has made that person confident enough to be more candid than those who joined you later and who feel less secure. Call on that person in Cabinet or briefings. Let others see it.

Use one-on-one meetings sparingly. It can become a bad habit to let ministers come and lobby you individually rather than make their case in front of others. But do use one-on-ones to give them feedback, either encouragement or a kick in the pants. Some people need more feedback than others, but all of them can come to feel that they aren't getting enough of your attention or that you don't understand what they are dealing with. There will be a tendency for ministers to realize that you spend a lot more time with certain people and to start to see these people as gatekeepers or buffers. A little bit of personal attention and active listening goes a long way toward preventing or postponing this perception from building up into resentment and toward keeping resentment from building up into danger.

Over time, your ministers and advisers will earn credibility with colleagues, and with you, by being right more often. If they anticipate the politics of a situation and have useful ideas about how to deal with it or if they raise a policy trade-off or implementation issue that turns out to be valid, their colleagues will be more likely to pay attention the next time. They will become the influencers.

You will not be successful if you hang on to the same closed circle of close advisers and confidants for your whole time in office. There is an inevitable drift into a comfort zone and a form of groupthink that can create blind spots and put you at risk. Sometimes, sudden departures come along – perhaps due to a political crisis or a personal choice to leave – and you lose one of your core team. But you will tend to want to stay with the people that you started with for too long, especially if your government is doing well. If you are doing badly in the polls, you can expect your ministers and caucus members to start grumbling about those in your inner circle and perhaps starting to spin against them with journalists. It can be a precursor to grumbling about you.

Succession planning is rarely done well in the political business, but try to pause at key points, perhaps during the summer recess of Parliament, and think about when would be the best time to swap out key players and who might be an option to bring in.

BEING THE PRIME MINISTER

The tenure of our prime ministers has ranged from a few months to twenty-one years. In the "modern era" of politics, the attention and the pressures are unrelenting, and at some point personal burnout and weariness by the electorate will set in. However long you hold the office, every week will be an opportunity to make a difference. If you are mindful of what you want to accomplish and pay attention to time management, to team dynamics, and to your own personal resilience, you will get a lot done and leave important legacies. Try not to govern one day at a time, fighting fires and feeding media cycles. Managing the short-term challenges is just a shield, one that lets you aim higher and bend the curve – of history.

4

ADVICE TO A MINISTER

There is nothing more important to understanding governing than understanding time. The one unbending, immovable constraint on a minister is that there is never enough time. Time is the finite resource in governing. A government can spend money it doesn't have on hand by borrowing. It can replenish or augment its political capital. It can put more people to work on problems. And it can add more processes of consultation and deliberation. What it cannot do is add to the 168 hours in a week or change the fact that it will have only so many weeks to use before the buzzer goes and it is time to face the voters again.

Being inside government feels different from being outside. It is a constant struggle to keep up, accompanied by a constant feeling that there are more things to do, more places to be, more things to read, and more people to talk to. The days feel long, yet the calendar flies by. Respite is brief, and the work stops only when you leave. Most people who leave governing feel that they have left projects incomplete and wish that they had done more.

YOUR TEAM

Your Advisers

As minister, you now have two sources of advice and support. One is your chief of staff and political office. The other is your deputy minister and the public service. The three of you form a triangle.

Effective ministers find a way to balance this triangle. That means not relying exclusively on one or the other, giving them roles that are complementary, keeping them in their swimming lanes, and encouraging a tone of civility, mutual respect, and candour between them.

Your political office shouldn't try to run the department, and your officials should stay far away from partisanship and political tactics. Your political staff can get themselves and you into trouble if they start messing around in the department's staffing or procurement. Your department will lose effectiveness if it starts to internalize current politics and drifts into telling you what you want to hear.

Keep in mind that your chief of staff and your deputy minister are working toward two objectives at the same time. The most important one is to assist and advise you and to make you successful. The other is to answer to and be coordinated by the "Centre" – the Prime Minister's Office and the Privy Council Office. Try to create an environment where they will let you know when they feel pulled in two directions. They will naturally want to hide their stress.

If you or the members of your political team develop friction with or lose confidence in one of the officials, you or the chief of staff should first take it up privately with the deputy minister. If you find that you have a serious issue with your deputy minister, ask to see the clerk and air it out.

Your Political Team

There was a time not so long ago when ministers could pick their own political staff, subject to a cap on how much they could spend on salaries for the office. They could pay them what they would accept, and there was always a supply of young, eager partisans ready to take on the jobs for modest pay and no job security. Working conditions tended to be exploitative and in some cases toxic.

Over time, some order has been imposed on how jobs are valued and paid; benchmarking to the nearby public service was an easy move. Some basic legal protections have recently been extended to people who work for members of Parliament and ministers. But the environment is still ripe for exploitation.

Ministers have seen their hiring discretion ebb as it has been displaced by the Prime Minister's Office. Modern practice is some variation of a double key, exercised formally or informally. The PMO may simply assign a chief of staff to you, or make a very strong suggestion that you will be brave to refuse, or perhaps retain a veto on your selection. It may allow your chief of staff to then fill out the other top jobs in your office, or it may impose other staff choices.

There is a rationale for this centralization. It is because the perspective of the PMO's staff is different. The Canadian Parliament isn't Congress. They will see a thirty-member Cabinet as a portfolio of assets to be developed over time. They will look at the supporting cast of political advisers the same way.

Although your political staff should not try to do the job of the public servants, there are crucial roles that only your political staff can play. They are part of a network composed of the staff of the other ministers, the staff of the prime minister, and the staff of your party's caucus. This network of a few hundred people will be led, loosely or tightly, by the chief of staff to the prime minister. Most political staff are constantly busy with their ministers and members of Parliament, so they don't easily get together. The most common management practice is a regular meeting of the chiefs of staff to the ministers with the PMO's senior staff, plus an occasional retreat-style gathering.

Your team will tend to develop more frequent and intense relations with some parts of the political network than others. It might be the political staff of the ministers from the same geographic part of the country or the staff of the ministers with whom your department does the most business. It will help you if your political team has good relations, or at least civil ones, with the staff of the minister of finance, the president of the Treasury Board, and the chairs of Cabinet committees that you will be attending. Occasional small favours or getting the benefit of the doubt will help you to keep your business moving forward. These offices can easily cause you grief through passive-aggressive resistance. These offices have been known to freeze out the ministers that they don't like and to make life easier for the ones that they do.

The members of your own team are the ones who will be constantly scanning for political danger, and opportunity, and the only ones who will be looking to enhance your standing among the pack.

They can take the raw material of speeches, announcements, social media posts, and media responses generated by the public service and add a dash of partisanship, a biting edge, or a personal touch when needed. Don't expect or ask the public service communications shops to do it.

Your staff should do the equivalent of advance work on all of the upcoming initiatives that you plan to take to Cabinet or into Parliament, meeting with other members of the government's political network to pitch, persuade, and gather feedback. Their outreach is an essential counterpart to the work done by your public service team through its own network. It is surprising how often this role is neglected or poorly executed.

Your staff can also cultivate stakeholders – not only by gathering useful input and making them feel heard but also by explaining your track record and advocating for your positions. Chances are that the stakeholders will be more direct with your staff than with you, and it helps to conserve your own time if they take on some of the load of meetings.

Every time you attend a meeting of the full caucus, some of your colleagues in Parliament will slip you a note asking you to give something your attention – usually on behalf of a constituent or a stakeholder. Opposition members will do the same. Your office can make sure that these requests are triaged and followed up. Ministers' offices usually set up VIP email addresses that they hand out only to caucus members or to all members of Parliament.

Your political staff will help you to fill out and manage the demands of the partisan side of your workload. You will be asked to add some heft to nomination meetings or constituency events for your colleagues in Parliament and to campaign during by-elections. You may have a formal role in the party apparatus that continues to work between elections. You will have fundraising targets to meet for yourself and for the party. Your staff will remind you of the demands of keeping the goodwill of the constituency that sent you to Ottawa and will push back against the department crowding them out of your schedule.

Your Deputy Minister

You will start off with one person who is your primary support from the public service. It is usually the obvious one – the deputy minister of the main department in the portfolio that you have been given. But it can be more complicated. You may have additional responsibilities that draw on other departments, or your scope may have been carved out from a big department or cobbled together. The clerk will have asked the senior deputy to sort out with colleagues the supply chain of support that you will need.

You don't need to like your deputy minister, but you need to be able to work with this person. Keep in mind that your deputy is highly motivated to see you succeed, or at least to keep you out of trouble. Open, honest, two-way communication is the key. It is not in your long-term interest to ignore or freeze out your deputy. Don't allow your office to start screening or filtering access by the deputy or blocking advice. Make sure to build in some time for your deputy to meet with you one-on-one or at least with just you and the chief of staff. Be direct about what kind of written briefings and meetings work best for you, but be open to making changes and pay special attention to the security briefings. The deputy will find a way to accommodate the many constraints on your schedule and your need to travel to your home constituency and on government business.

Your Parliamentary Team
The prime minister will assign one of your caucus colleagues to be your parliamentary secretary. You might even have two of them or share one with another minister. You won't have a say. This colleague is chosen primarily to complement or counterbalance you – the yin to your yang – with regard to region, gender, language, or some other factor. You may or may not like or get along with this person. Parliamentary

secretaries tend to be chosen from either the ambitious up-and-comers or the veterans. Their appointment may be seen by the PMO as an apprenticeship or development opportunity or as a consolation prize.

You will want to be very deliberate and work out the role that the parliamentary secretary can play for you. Don't leave it to chance. This person's job is to help you to be effective, and your parliamentary secretary's prospects for advancement are now intertwined with your success. Find a way to fit this colleague in. It is a common mistake by ministers to underuse what a parliamentary secretary can bring.

Practice regarding parliamentary secretaries changes with prime ministers. In some governments, parliamentary secretaries are given some of the tools of the minister, such as the clearance to read Cabinet papers or classified documents. Sometimes, they are not. In any case, these colleagues have access to closed meetings of your party's caucus and regional caucus and to the closed meetings of parliamentary committees, and they can become a valued source of political intelligence.

What you are seeking is a strong triangle and cordial working relations among the parliamentary secretary, the legislative team in your political office, and the parliamentary affairs team in your department. The parliamentary secretary can be a useful link to the government

House leader, to the government's lead in the Senate, and to whatever group is coordinating the government's overall parliamentary agenda.

First and foremost, the parliamentary secretary can help you to gather intelligence and to manage relations with your parliamentary committees, the caucus, and senators. This person can help you to advance your bills in a number of ways. Your parliamentary secretary will have more time and a front-line seat. This will help you to identify where tweaks and amendments would improve the bill or reduce resistance. A parliamentary secretary can haggle over timelines and witness schedules and over the wording of motions and committee reports.

This colleague may be allowed to play defence for you in Question Period when you are away and can make sure that you meet your obligations to table documents in Parliament. Your parliamentary secretary can help with the quarterbacking on days when you are unlucky enough to be the target of an Opposition Day debate.

It is up to you whether you want to give your parliamentary secretary a wider role, representing you at events away from Parliament Hill or on panel and pundit shows. It is a relatively low-risk way to cover more ground. This colleague can be a useful complement to your style, being combative so that you can be conciliatory or vice versa, or you can switch back and forth as needed.

CABINET

You have two ways to influence Cabinet. One is to do a good job presenting your own proposals, and the other is to make useful and persuasive interventions regarding those of your colleagues. In either case, being concise helps – less is more – so keep your remarks tight and to the point. Don't intervene all the time, or colleagues may start to tune you out. You will want to cultivate a reputation as someone who should be listened to because you know your stuff. That means not only showing a command of your portfolio's subject matter but also having insight into the politics surrounding it and your part of Canada.

Cabinet is always subject to group dynamics. Some colleagues have more presence and bigger personalities, some love to tell anecdotes or leaven the mood with witty remarks, some are surly and uncommunicative, and some are insecure and quick to defer to others. There are often strong underlying currents of regional politics, of past leadership contests, or old turf wars between federal departments that are not easy to detect just reading the formal Cabinet papers. As time goes by, you will recognize the patterns and get better at reading the room.

You should pick a small team from your political staff and the public service that you trust to give you candid advice on upcoming Cabinet business. If you present something, you will be accompanied by at least one person from your political staff and one senior official who knows the file. They will see how it goes and learn from it – unless you trigger one of those rare discussions where the prime minister asks that the room be cleared. For other parts of the meeting, you won't be accompanied, and you will have to be very sparing and careful in telling anyone anything so as to preserve Cabinet secrecy and to make it less likely that you will be culpable in any leak investigation. Give your team feedback on what kind of presentations and briefings work best for you. Even a quick verbal briefing the morning of a Cabinet or Cabinet committee meeting can go a long way and supplement whatever written material has been prepared.

YOUR MANDATE

The Mandate Letter
One of the first things that you should do is to sit down with your deputy minister and your chief of staff and go through the mandate letter in detail. Ask them for some sort of planning meeting with attendance from both sides of the triangle so that you can start laying out how, together, you are going to get everything in the

> " One of the first things that you
> should do is to sit down with your
> deputy minister and your chief
> of staff and go through the
> mandate letter in detail. "

mandate done. As currently used, a mandate letter contains the prime minister's instructions to you about what you should be trying to accomplish and how you should conduct yourself – the "what" and the "how." It usually has no explicit timelines or expiry date but is valid for the rest of the government's parliamentary mandate or until it is overwritten by a new one.

The mandate letter has been an evolving part of Canadian governance. Not that long ago, it didn't exist. A minister would have to infer a list of tasks from the party's electoral platform and from the government's first Speech from the Throne, blended with the briefings provided by the department on what business could be forecast. This is still the practice in some provincial governments.

Written instructions from the prime minister were initially treated as highly confidential, akin to Cabinet papers and shared only with a selected few within government. Then some governments began to publish them in the early days after swearing in a Cabinet, raising expectations for others to do the same.

Publishing mandate letters is not without cost and risk. They give the Opposition, stakeholders, and media pundits clear signals and a jump on working out how to resist you. They create a scorecard on how many of your tasks you accomplish and on how many tasks the government as a team accomplishes, a scorecard that can easily be used to question your competence or to accuse you of "broken promises."

Nevertheless, the letters have proven to be useful to ministers and especially to prime ministers. The natural drift of governing is to be reactive from week to week to events and external forces. After a government has made its first handful of opening moves, it can easily lose momentum, traction, or direction.

Mandate letters can push back against this drift and can make sure that ministers don't dissipate the initial energy and political capital that they enjoy on day one. The letters contribute to traction and make it more likely that the government will start to rack up accomplishments in the second and third year and have something to present to electors.

The letters are a useful complement to the Speech from the Throne, which is a few thousand words delivered in a formal setting and tone by the governor general. Mandate letters are in the voice of the prime minister, and they help the Clerk of the Privy Council to organize the public service and help the prime minister's chief of staff to organize the political network because they carry the prime minister's authority.

For each minister, the letter also serves as a sort of gyroscope to get you back on course. You will inevitably have to respond and react. This is the day-to-day trade of "issue management." Issue management can boil up into full-blown "crisis management," which can consume all of your time and focus. Mandate letters are readily transformed into work plans, ensuring that while you are busy in reactive mode, others are working on your proactive initiatives as best they can. When the crisis passes, you will know what you are supposed to get back to advancing.

Mandate letters can also serve to sort out potential overlap and friction among ministers. Many issues draw on more than one minister. Sorting out which minister has the lead and which ministers are expected to pitch in can reduce friction costs and enhance the productivity of the team. However, don't be surprised if the letters actually create points of ambiguity that will have to be worked out.

Mandate letters send signals and messages to stakeholders. They can reassure allies and help backbenchers. They can create at least some pressure on the Opposition to declare its position or alternative. But don't count on it; overwhelmingly, the spotlight is on you. There is far less onus on the Opposition to have a positive program than there is on you.

There is no fixed template for mandate letters. If the text is too detailed, they may create unrealistic deadlines and limit options and due diligence. So they are usually written as statements of intent or direction and are meant to serve as a bridge to the actual work planning and decision making.

If you have been moved from one portfolio to another, you may not get a fresh mandate letter for a while, and you will be expected to pick up where your predecessor left off. Your successor in your old department may be going through the same experience.

Status, Influence, Power

The influence or "power" of a minister is not easy to assess, despite many attempts by journalists to create ranking scores. Some portfolios inherently carry with them the potential to affect outcomes and to affect other colleagues – notably finance. Tradition says that some of the assignments are "senior." But that can be deceptive. Sometimes, one of those supposedly senior ministers is actually kept on a very short leash by the prime minister, who will make the major decisions and grab the big events, whereas other ministers with seemingly junior portfolios seem to carry the day in Cabinet or at budget time. Being the president of the Treasury Board or the chair of a Cabinet committee is another way to exert influence, provided you do it reasonably well, but it is not a role that will draw much attention from those watching from outside of the government and tends to be underestimated in media rankings.

Think of a solar system with the prime minister at the centre. Some people will be in closer orbits than others and will have more proximity or more access. The difference is that in this solar system, you can move from the outer to the inner circles – and vice versa. You have almost no influence on which specific portfolio you will be assigned or on how long you will stay there, but your performance and your conduct can affect how valuable you are to the team and your status within it.

One path to greater influence is to earn your colleagues' respect as an astute politician with good judgment and advice about how to make winning arguments and how to thwart your team's opponents. Another is to develop a reputation for having an indisputable grasp of how issues and messages will play out in your part of the country or with certain stakeholder communities. Influence is gained not just at the Cabinet table but also at meetings of your party's caucus, at other smaller gatherings of your political teammates, and at meetings that the

> One path to greater influence is to earn your colleagues' respect as an astute politician with good judgment and advice about how to make winning arguments and how to thwart your team's opponents.

prime minister may convene on particular topics.

Knowing your stuff in your own portfolio and delivering for the team – getting things done, giving your colleagues team accomplishments to talk about, and staying out of unnecessary trouble – are essential to thriving in the long run.

Some combination of these elements creates the real "power index," one that will rise and fall over time. In politics and governing, you will accumulate the equivalent of the campaign bars issued by the military to its officers. Pay no attention to the media report cards and indexes. They are not the prime minister.

Funding Programs

Many ministers are assigned portfolios that flow money to people and groups outside of the government. Billions of dollars go out in

> " Contributions are the work-
> horse tool of many parts of
> government. "

"Gs and Cs" – grants and contributions. Contributions are the workhorse tool of many parts of government. Money is provided for a purpose and with conditions, and recipients have to report what they do with it and perhaps to repay some or all of it.

Funding programs, especially contribution programs, is an area where you need to tread very carefully. You do have the right to influence where the funding flows to from the programs for which you are answerable. Ultimately, it is your authority that is being exercised in most funding programs, and you will feel a degree of ownership of the programs once you have been asked about them in Question Period or at committee. But it is easy to be accused of "political interference."

Early on, you will be asked whether you want to delegate to officials some or all of your decision-making power for various categories of expenditure. Similarly, if the department or its agencies have regulatory functions, you may also be asked to sign off on the delegation of some regulatory decisions to officials. These "charts of delegations" can be updated and amended any time, and you should ask for at least an annual checkup. Each portfolio is different, and a few departments come with a large array of programs that require thousands of decisions every year.

You face a trade-off as minister: the less you delegate to others, the more time and effort you will have to put into "signing time," especially at certain times of the year. More importantly, the less buffer you will then have from the outcomes. In cases where trouble erupts, it will be easier for you to overrule an official than to reverse yourself. But the more you delegate, the more you have to trust that the officials are doing more or less what you would want to be doing.

A degree of buffering is preferable, as it isn't in your interest to be seen as personally involved. The community of potential applicants and recipients, as well as applicants for regulatory permits and licences, and their paid lobbyists, will quickly adapt and start pestering you and your political staff, trying to fast-forward timelines or overrule the processes for allocation and approval.

Most funding programs are oversubscribed, and a lot of the applicants will be rejected or get less than they hoped for. Many regulatory programs create winners and losers. They will be less likely to grumble and complain or to lash out and start stoking Opposition and media critics if you can point to a process that is plausibly arm's length from you and that is following objective criteria.

Whatever the temptation, there isn't much room for you or your staff to be involved. Practice has evolved to require that every single funding agreement and every single contract, above some minimal threshold, be posted on the Internet. There are people out there combing the disclosure lists and digging further if they see something interesting. For some of them, it is their business as information brokers. If you or your staff leave fingerprints, they will be found.

But this doesn't mean that you are powerless. You can and should take an interest in the design of any program that you answer for – the criteria that will be used to determine basic eligibility, the factors that will be used to assess or rank applicants, their relative weight, and the areas where discretion and judgment will have to be exercised by officials. These details can all be changed.

Ask to see lists of past recipients. Ask what the success-failure ratio of applications has been. There is probably an evaluation or audit of the program that you or you staff could take a look at. Ask if one is scheduled over the next couple of years, as the findings will come out on your watch.

If you aren't satisfied that any funding program is sufficiently aligned with where you want to go, then change it. But it would be better to aim to change it before the next intake round of applications than to intervene in the current one. It may take a bit of time and effort, but ultimately you can work something out. In the end, you could generate a useful "announceable" to deploy later. Minor changes are within your power. You may have to go and get permission from the Treasury Board if the change is big enough, and you may even have to go to Cabinet. But if you have a good case for how you are going to make the program better, you will usually prevail. Just remember one important point: you won't be able to get more money for the program without jumping through the obstacle course that is the budget.

THE CLOCK IS RUNNING

Blocking Out Your Time

From the day of your swearing-in, there are many potential uses of your precious days and hours as a minister. Deciding how to allocate each one means deciding not to do something else. No two ministers will face exactly the same mix, but all are pulled into many roles.

In the House of Commons, you'll be required to fulfill a quota of "House duty" hours. You

> " ... you won't be able to get more money for the program without jumping through the obstacle course that is the budget. "

must be there for some of the debates and almost all votes.

As a member of the governing party's caucus, you will attend national gatherings (traditionally on Wednesday mornings in parallel with meetings of the other parties' caucuses) as well as gatherings of one of the regional caucuses (which are often held as breakfast meetings), and you will take meetings with your colleagues in Parliament.

In Question Period, even though it takes place five times a week during sitting weeks, you may go days or weeks without being asked anything. But you may find yourself the piñata of the week and have to spend extra hours rehearsing or working on damage control. You are expected to be there for most of them. Some journalists will be keeping track of attendance.

As an answerable minister, you will appear before House and Senate committees to advocate for your legislation, to answer for your appropriations, or to discuss your part in whatever matters are hot topics at the time.

As a member of Cabinet, you will find yourself attending full Cabinet meetings and sitting on at least one or two Cabinet committees. That means finding time to read some of the flow of documents containing your colleagues' proposals (there could be dozens each week), or at least some sort of briefing note about them. If you show some talent, you will probably be asked to chair a Cabinet committee, and then you will definitely need to read more and find more time for pre-meeting briefings.

As the minister of a portfolio, probably one with a core department and a constellation of satellite agencies, you will be asked for feedback and direction. Be prepared for constant pressure to fill every hour with meetings and events and documents to read.

As the Member of Parliament for a constituency, you will be expected to be there for constituents and local events, available in your office both as a sort of ombudsperson for their interactions with government and as a future candidate raising your local profile and cultivating the local base of the donors, volunteers, and voters you will need next time.

> *As the member of a family and a human being*
> *trying to be healthy, you will find yourself*
> *making excuses and apologies; this is the*
> *area that very often suffers.*

The sum of these demands will always exceed the available hours. Which of them do you think is most likely to be crowded out?

When the House is sitting and once you fill in the "must dos" such as Question Period, caucus meetings, Cabinet time, and House duty, about half your week will be spoken for. Another large slice of time will be dedicated to the portfolio that you have been assigned. There will always be more people to meet, more things to read, more places to go. You will be playing at the margins of your schedule until you leave office.

The art of being a successful minister lies in mindful, purposeful allocation of packets of your time.

Some weeks in frosty Ottawa will feel like a biathlon but with people shooting back. A big risk for any minister is burnout. It will take reserves of discipline to nourish personal relationships and to maintain physical and mental well-being. You are now at an elevated risk of divorce and estrangement from your children.

The default settings of ministerial life can grind you down – bad diet, too much coffee or alcohol, not enough sleep, shifts in time zones.

> " The art of being a successful minister lies in mindful, purposeful allocation of packets of your time. "

You won't be around for your partner, children, or parents. Fatigue will push you to become irritable and reactive. There is a reason why the tone and demeanour in Parliament deteriorate as the long session from January to the summer wears on.

Whereas other people may get away from their jobs on weekends or during school breaks or may find recovery strategies that work for them – exercise, meditation, team sports, hobbies, socializing, quiet time, family dinners, travel – none of these strategies will be available to you unless you very consciously protect time for them.

Although you may be able to limit your House and departmental duties to the traditional core workweek, it is precisely the weekend and break weeks that the party and constituency office will want to fill with political activities – whether undertaken in your own constituency or while helping out colleagues in others. You may find yourself on a relentless loop of travel back to the riding almost every

> Living by yourself in Ottawa
> is the worst option.

weekend for months at a time. If you are successful and stay in Cabinet, it can go on for years.

There is no right answer to the question of whether to bring the family to Ottawa or leave them at home. It will depend on your own constellation, what is best for them, how long it takes you to get home, and whether you can find a congenial housemate or two. Living by yourself in Ottawa is the worst option.

Your Scheduling Assistants
One of the first things that you must do is to exert an iron grip on who is authorized to allocate your time. For that, you will need a strong-minded but tactful scheduling assistant. If you already have someone from the past, all the better, but the routines of a minister's offices can be very different from anything that you have experienced, so do not hesitate to upgrade your scheduling assistant if it doesn't work out. There will be potential friction between the assistants in your Parliament Hill office, the departmental office, and the constituency office, so make sure that they sort out the protocols early.

Some ministers lose control of their time because their own team overprograms them. One assistant will be pressing for you to do media interviews or to create social media posts. The constituency office will be clamouring for you to attend events back home. Another will want you to work on persuading caucus members to support an upcoming initiative. Another will have stakeholders clamouring for a meeting or for you to attend their event. A weak chief of staff will struggle to sort out these pressures.

You will need to regularly review the forward schedule and adjust the mix to recover the balance that you will need over the long haul. You can help yourself by not trying to do your own scheduling and by not overcommitting your time to people you run into. Send them all to talk to your ministerial office. Protect your flexibility.

It won't hurt to pause after you have acquired some more experience to re-examine your own go-to preferences. Check whether you have unconsciously created a comfort zone from which you reluctantly stray, and try to make adjustments.

Travel

You won't have complete control of your schedule, especially if you intend to leave Ottawa. The Prime Minister's Office keeps a watchful eye on the deployment of the ministerial team, and

> " You can help yourself by not trying to do your own scheduling and by not overcommitting your time to people you run into. "

the government whip will be checking to make sure that enough ministers are around for House duty or votes. Votes are normally kept within a Monday to Thursday window, often late in the day, but there will be exceptions and surprises.

Each administration puts in place some mechanism to screen ministerial travel. You may just have to regularly send in a forward calendar, or you may need a more specific clearance, especially for travel outside the country, of which the Department of Global Affairs will also keep track. Your office will be kept informed of shifting parliamentary obligations, and your office may have to do some trading with other ministers to free you up.

You may also find travel added to your schedule if the PMO assigns you to do "outreach" – such as helping to market an initiative led by one of your colleagues, accompanying the prime minister, or making announcements or attending events that help out one of your party's caucus members or candidates. In fact, others will be annoyed if you travel to some part of Canada without checking for opportunities to help out the team.

THE THEATRE OF ANSWERABILITY

Parliamentary Appearances

One of the core principles of Canadian government is the answerability of ministers to Parliament, and you should take this principle very seriously. Most Canadians see ministers in the particular frame of Question Period. Less frequently, they see them at parliamentary committees or in open debate in the House.

As a minister, you have interests and a perspective on Question Period that are now quite different. Question Period is almost entirely driven by highly topical issues in the news cycle and is dominated by attempts to expose shortcomings in the government's performance. For ministers, it is a defensive exercise with very little upside. For you, a boring Question Period is a win.

You may be familiar as a Member of Parliament with appearances by ministers at House of Commons committees. Indeed each spring, two unlucky ministers are singled out for an appearance at the Committee of the Whole – an extended grilling by the entire House of Commons. Fewer Canadians will see you at a House or Senate committee, but you will be watched by some journalists and interested

> " One of the core principles of Canadian government is the answerability of ministers to Parliament, and you should take this principle very seriously. "

stakeholders, and there is at least some scope for you to actually get your messages across.

There are two main reasons why you will find yourself at a House or Senate committee. One is to shepherd a government bill. The other is to present your department's request for spending authority.

Presenting Bills. Ministers are typically the first witnesses invited to speak at the committee review stage that follows second reading. It will be you or your officials presenting the bill. Less frequently, ministers are called back at the end of the committee stage, after all the other witnesses have been heard, when the committee starts to focus on possible amendments. Speaking first at the committee stage is an opportunity for you to state the case for the bill and to respond to a round or two of questions that go over the points of resistance already revealed in the second-reading debate.

In any parliamentary appearance, there can be a genuine exchange of perspectives with other parliamentarians that brings to light areas where amendments will improve the bill. The committee appearances serve to keep Canadians informed, as these discussions will be disseminated on the Internet and will be recorded and posted.

But very few people will watch live unless you are the particularly hot topic of the week or the day. Stakeholders and most journalists will go back and watch the discussion later online or read the Hansard transcript. Even for hot topics, a couple of minutes at most will show up on the news shows that day.

Appearing at committee is mostly about you or the Opposition getting things on the record that can be useful when spinning to the media, engaging stakeholders, preparing social media posts, or even fundraising for the party. It may be a turn of phrase, or a visual clip, or just a photo of your facial expression. The Opposition may want to create a useful clip of one of its team delivering its message. You may want to get this person on the record opposing your bill or program and later use these words against the Opposition.

For bills that are relatively noncontentious or generally popular, the Opposition will try to get you to make amendments, and then it will try to take credit for them. The Opposition may be playing a longer game, trying to set up an implementation issue so that it can come back months or years later with a version of "we told you so" and attack your competence. Nevertheless, don't let partisanship make you too defensive. There is a good chance that valid points or arguments have been made and you should be willing to accommodate them.

Approval of Spending. Parliamentary approval of spending is one of the core principles of Westminster government. However, ministers' appearances that relate to the spending estimates are rarely about the actual estimates. The committee will be able to interrogate officials about the specific line items if it seeks details. An appearance by the minister provides a platform to grill you on any topic more or less related to your portfolio, usually the most current hot issues, or to probe you for some weakness that makes you look out of touch or not on top of your files.

Whether your party has a majority or not, don't underprepare. Make it easier for your government colleagues on a House committee or for your allies in the Senate by ensuring that they don't have to spend time and energy rescuing you or covering for your shortcomings. Take the time to go over the material that your department and political staff have prepared. Create a time slot for a preparatory briefing.

You will want memory jogs and prompts prepared in a particular format or easy-to-read font. Never try to improvise and answer on the fly; say that you will be happy to get back to the committee with the answer or that committee members can ask the officials.

Don't be overconfident. You may come through a dozen appearances successfully, each one a safe crossing, and be torpedoed at the next. This is the one that people will remember.

Think of it as performance and be mindful of tone and body language. There are specialized coaches who can go over recordings of practice sessions or past appearances and give you feedback and tips. No matter how provoked, you want to project calm and civility. You want to appear serious and deferential to parliamentary process, even if some of the parliamentarians behave badly and get under your skin. Don't take the bait; don't try to win an exchange. Boring and forgettable is just fine.

For a minister, it is all about defence – not being scored against or not creating new ammunition for the Opposition. The only parliamentary committee appearances that are remembered days or weeks later are the ones where ministers were successfully hit or where they looked to be flustered, irritable, or in over their heads. You have far more to lose than the Opposition members.

> You may come through a dozen appearances successfully, each one a safe crossing, and be torpedoed at the next. This is the one that people will remember.

Appearing before a Senate committee is generally less personal and partisan in tone but carries a different risk. It is far more likely that you will run across senators who have deep backgrounds in particular areas, who are more likely to have done a lot of homework before your appearance, and who are more likely to have strong views that may be difficult to shift. You will have to be on top of your files. You will want to make it easier for other senators to support your bill by feeding them good arguments.

LIVING IN A GLASS HOUSE

Accountability

Modern practice, which has been shaped by the cumulative responses to some painful experiences by previous governments, is to routinely and proactively disclose almost all of the outputs of government decision making as well as many of its intermediate inputs.

Annual audited financial statements, pulled together as public accounts, are supplemented by quarterly statements and monthly updates. Bills and the resulting laws are published. Regulations and executive orders are posted in the *Canada Gazette* (creating the verb "to gazette"). Itemized spending on travel and hospitality by a wide swath of "public office holders" is posted. Lists of government contracts are posted. Lists of grants and contributions and the recipients are posted. Audits and evaluations of programs are posted. Appointments are posted. Taxpayer-funded polling is released. People who meet with you to "lobby" have to disclose that they did so.

On top of all this proactive disclosure, you will have to be responsive to written questions submitted by members of Parliament, to requests from parliamentary committees and officers of Parliament, and to requests to see records under both the Access to Information Act and the Privacy Act. You and your department may have to provide documents or depositions as the defendant in court cases.

This web of transparency serves its broader purpose of improving Canadian governance by enabling the Opposition, institutional watchdogs, the media, stakeholders, and the public to hold you to account.

The result of this trend to greater transparency is that the zone where the Opposition and media can play "gotcha" has shifted over the years. So have the parameters of what constitutes a scandal. And so have the criteria for what is still confidential or secret.

Criminality in the form of fraud, breach of trust, misappropriation of public moneys for personal gain, interference in judicial, prosecutorial, or police matters, and interference or cheating in elections – all of these are now very rare in Canada. Consequently, any whiff of it is very exciting and is likely to generate a frenzy. The usual first move by the Opposition will be to write to the RCMP or to an officer of Parliament demanding an investigation. Even if the Opposition doesn't really believe that the investigation will bear fruit, it will at least get to label you and your government as "under investigation."

All to say that you have very strong incentives not just to behave legally but also to behave correctly – above reproach. You will have been given a copy of the government's guidebook on these matters. Read it, study it, and ask questions if you aren't clear on something. You can seek advice on how to stay out of trouble from several sources – including from your deputy minister, from the clerk, or even confidentially from one of the officers of Parliament.

> " All to say that you have very strong incentives not just to behave legally but also to behave correctly – above reproach. "

Leak, or Is It Spin?

Because so many outputs and intermediate inputs are now routinely made public, what are always of great interest to people outside of government are the inputs and the deliberative discussions that take place before decisions are made. Lots of people want to find out what the advice was, perhaps what the options and factors were when you made a decision, as well as who had your ear.

Because of the central importance in Westminster government of caucus and Cabinet discussions, they want to know who took what view.

Some of this curiosity is benign; there are people who are simply interested in politics and government. Some people sincerely believe in maximum transparency.

Much of the curiosity is less noble. Canadian stakeholders, interest groups, and foreign governments want this information in order to increase their ability to apply pressure on the government and to advance their own interests. Most commonly, their immediate interest is to block a course of action by stirring up resistance and forcing the government to take it off the table as an option.

You should always be very wary in speaking to journalists or to Opposition politicians. One of the most common errors made by ministers is to overestimate their skill with this type of exchange or to underestimate the risk. Opposition politicians and many journalists have careers or personal agendas that can be advanced by inflicting damage on governments and their ministers. You will do just fine as one of their trophies, and they can be merciless, however cordial or friendly they have seemed in the past. Other politicians and journalists are less personally motivated, but the nature of their job is that they are relentless in looking for what could have or should have been done differently. They will always have the advantage of hindsight.

So what is a "leak" these days? A leak is often about the period before a decision. Westminster government works best when there is a space or zone for candid and frank debate and discussion about a wide array of options and considerations in the period leading up to a decision. This discussion could be between ministers and their officials and staff, among ministers at the Cabinet table, among members of Parliament

> " You should always be very wary in speaking to journalists or to Opposition politicians. One of the most common errors made by ministers is to overestimate their skill with this type of exchange or to underestimate the risk. "

at a caucus meeting, or among officials. This debate and discussion could be embedded in the content of a meeting, a document, or a trail of email and text exchanges.

"Leaks" before decisions are made often do damage and disrupt this pre-decision debate. They can prematurely shrink the range of options, discourage risk taking, and pre-empt the ability of ministers to make their case in a manner and timing of their own choosing. Leaks erode trust and solidarity and reduce future candour.

Truly accidental leaks, in the sense of a burst pipe, are very rare – and therefore memorable. You can reduce the risk to close to zero. There is no excuse for leaving sensitive documents, probably stored on a laptop or tablet, in hotel rooms or on airplanes or in the trunk of your car. Being "hacked" is more common, and you probably won't know it happened at the time.

You should always assume that people will be trying to intercept your electronic communications or overhear your conversations in airport lounges, on airplanes, and in restaurants. Conduct yourself accordingly. Make sure that you get an early briefing on security and cybersecurity and take it seriously. Many leaks are caused by carelessness. Ministerial staffers and mid-level public servants sometimes reveal more than they should as they try to impress others by appearing to be in the loop and in the know.

Most serious "leaks" are intentional and have a purpose. Many leaks come from the government side, and the intention is "positive" – to get something out and moving forward before the forces of opposition and resistance can mobilize. Someone on the government side may be leaking about something that the government intends to do in order to cultivate "friendly" stakeholders or journalists. A leak may be a very deliberate tactical move – a "trial balloon," to use an old metaphor – meant to test the reception that an initiative is going to get while there is time to delay or to modify the initiative or the launch. Here, a leak enters the realm of "spin."

Other times, the purpose of a leak within government may be "negative" – a way to block something, perhaps something the government intends to do, without having to stand up and take responsibility. Especially if the government is under stress, it could be a member of your own political team, a backbench caucus member or staff in another minister's office, who is leaking to block you.

Many of the leaks from the public service or military are not "whistle-blowing" or even attempts to nudge decisions but rather a clumsy attempt by someone in the middle layers to create pressure on the government to allocate more resources by giving the media and the Opposition tools to go after the government.

Career-Ending Moves

Standards of conduct have steadily improved – mostly because norms have changed in society but also because the chances of being called out or caught have gone up. Behaviours that were common in the 1990s would now trigger calls for resignation in the 2020s. Consequently, aberrations stand out even more.

One of the surefire ways that a ministerial career can end abruptly is because of a behavioural transgression. You should conduct yourself on the assumption that in the end anything and everything is likely to be revealed. Months of your work on legislation or programs will likely be long forgotten, whereas stories of harassment complaints or entitlement to taxpayers' dollars can live on for years after you are gone.

> " One of the surefire ways that a ministerial career can end abruptly is because of a behavioural transgression. "

There was a time, not that long ago, when overt bullying and sexual harassment were part of the culture of many political offices of ministers and members of Parliament. Gossip on the Hill knew who the "difficult bosses" and the "hounds" were, and many a colleague or journalist would turn a blind eye. Over time, the threshold has shifted dramatically, bad behaviour has become rarer, and the consequences are now much harsher. Poor conduct is one of the fastest ways to end your career.

Canadian politics has an extremely low threshold for use of public funds compared to other democracies. You should assume that there are people out there who would love to trip you up. There is a small industry scanning for transgressions by trawling web postings, filing Access to Information requests, and peddling the results to media outlets or advocacy groups. Nuggets will be seized upon by the Opposition and by journalists looking for the big score to advance their own standing. Every year, there will be a predictable cycle of news stories revealing who spent how much on travel, meals, or office renovations, or even better, who travelled on government aircraft or travelled outside of Canada.

It is one of those permanent realities of Canada that in a country that spans six time zones, has spotty access beyond the major centres, and has a dismal rail service, you can't make use of a government aircraft or a chartered aircraft without bringing down scorn and theatrical outrage. So don't do it unless as a last resort. Yes, you could gain time relative to commercial travel, and you could do some work or have a candid conversation without worrying about who is in the airport lounge or in the seat behind you, but don't do it.

Your staff can protect you by ensuring that you stay well inside the boundaries or by putting the bill for the meal on one of their credit cards, the reimbursments to be sorted out later. You can protect yourself by setting the default in your office at frugal and picking up the small stuff out of your own pocket. Don't give anyone the chance to put the "entitled" label on you; once it sticks, it is hard to get off.

Your own career can be damaged by transgressions by your staffers. When they mess up, it will lead to an inquisition along the lines of "what did you know and when did you know it?" You can't win. Either as minister you knew and condoned it, or as minister you didn't act

> " You can protect yourself by setting the default in your office at frugal ... "

quickly enough, or as minister you didn't know, proving that you were oblivious and out of touch. Lay down high expectations for your staff to stay out of trouble.

It doesn't matter that much that Parliament has created arm's-length processes to assess and rule on alleged transgressions – a commissioner on ethics and conflict of interest and a commissioner on lobbying, for example. There's also a Board of Internal Economy to deal with conduct issues on the Hill. These processes take time, and they won't deflect Opposition members or the media if they see an opportunity to hurt you. Indeed, in recent years, all parties have developed the ploy of writing to one of these "watchdogs" demanding an investigation. It works well for them. None of the watchdogs can refuse to at least conduct some fact-finding before dismissing a complaint, and most will happily take on the file because their status in the Ottawa firmament requires them to appear to be busy. That gives your critics a valuable window to label you as "under investigation." The more investigations, the better. As though drilling for oil, they are always hoping for a gusher among the dry wells.

Don't expect any benefit of the doubt or presumption of innocence. Even if you develop a cordial working relationship with your immediate critic or the members of your relevant parliamentary committee, it won't protect you. Someone on the other side is there ready to climb over the boards and punch you in the face.

Legal Challenges

You may or may not be a lawyer, but there is a good chance that you are going to use one. Some portfolios use a lot of them, of different varieties. Some places need a lot of transactional legal services to make sure that contracts, leases, funding agreements, and other administrative matters are done correctly. Some use lawyers to negotiate or to help negotiating teams. Some seek legal advice within their policy and regulatory activities to reduce the risk that a law, regulation, or policy is badly

> " Don't expect any benefit of the doubt or presumption of innocence. "

drafted and to make it less exposed to successful challenge in the courts. Canada's lawmakers will always check on "Charter risk," something that their counterparts in the United Kingdom and Australia don't have to worry about.

You will be challenged. You may find it unsettling at first to read in your news feed that someone has sued your department or taken one of your decisions to court. The initial spin in the news stories will be heavily against you, as they instinctively adopt a "David versus Goliath" narrative. Sometimes the plaintiff's lawyers will try to personalize the story, naming you directly or threatening to get you in the stand. You can expect the Opposition to pile on.

Don't let it get to you. Litigation is just one of the tools that people use to try to achieve their goals, and there are thousands of actions against the government every year. Some have merit, and some are just long-shot attempts to try to score a settlement.

As long as you have gone about your duties in good faith and have not tried to benefit yourself or someone close to you, you will be considered as acting for the Crown and be defended by the Crown's lawyers. This access to legal assistance will be there for you as a former minister if the case drags on, but that won't likely come up, as in practice the next minister will take the baton and inherit the case.

> " The Opposition will always side with the plaintiffs and try to put you in the worst possible light. The initial media coverage will always amplify the case against you. "

If you are sued, there can be a natural divergence among how you see a case, how your department sees it, and how the lawyers see it. You may instinctively want the perception of conflict to go away and want to settle. Indeed, few ministers have the stomach for a high-profile fight with a media-savvy stakeholder group. The Opposition will always side with the plaintiffs and try to put you in the worst possible light. The initial media coverage will always amplify the case against you. You will have the harder case to make in terms of messaging. However, a good fight with a provincial government or special interest group that is trying to block one of your policies may help you politically by giving you opportunities to make your case to the broader public.

If a litigation case is big enough, either in financial terms or policy and politics implications, you will probably have to go to the Treasury Board or some other committee of

Cabinet and make the case for settling, or for refusing to settle. Some ministers see settlements as a perfectly good "announceable," especially if they can blame a previous government for getting into the mess. The department is more likely to want to defend itself, especially if it is at risk of having to absorb the cost of the settlement. The lawyers often see a point of law worth fighting for, even if it will take more time and energy and prolong the political pain. This view may be shared by the senior lawyers at the Department of Justice, who will be keeping a watchful eye on how case law is evolving and looking further down the road. In contrast, the Department of Finance and the Treasury Board may be happy to get something trimmed from the contingent liability that they have to disclose on the government's financial statements. Just don't get out ahead of them, or you may be digging a financial hole.

Sometimes, ministers or their staff want to get involved in picking the legal team, and they often assume that "outside counsel" from private law firms will do a better job or that bringing in a "ringer" like a retired judge will help. Maybe but maybe not. You may have picked up grumbles or sniping from private sector lawyers regarding the federal Department of Justice, but it is actually a very good law firm with some very good lawyers. In any case, it is the minister of justice who is the government's attorney (the attorney general in American terminology), and through the Department of Justice, this minister will decide who represents the government. The minister of justice manages the in-house staff and a roster of outside help that can be retained, especially when specialized knowledge is needed. You can be a well-informed and engaged client, but you will have to yield to the Department of Justice.

Given the volume of litigation against the government and the hundreds of active cases working their way up through the lower courts toward appeal courts, there is a good chance that on your watch there will be a few court rulings that disrupt your agenda. It could be an injunction blocking a regulatory decision or the awarding of damages. It might be a decision that strikes down and renders inoperable some regulation, some piece of a law, or an entire law, which will add to your "to-do list" and may divert effort and attention away from the tasks in your mandate letter. You should ask your department staff from time to time, at least once a year, for their best forward scan of the potential impact that the courts could have.

PLAYING THE GAME TO WIN

Performance Reports
The prime minister and the PMO will have formed an initial view of the strengths and

weaknesses of each member of the team during the transition period between the election and the swearing-in of Cabinet. The team is never a completely blank slate. Along with the prime minister, the staff will know some people better than others from prior encounters, perhaps in Opposition, during the leadership race, or from life before politics. They may see any given minister as a defeated rival, a key ally, or a potential future threat.

Never forget that the PMO is fiercely loyal to the current prime minister and that if the staff feel threatened, they will attempt to cut potential threats down to size. They will always put the needs of the prime minister ahead of yours in assigning and reassigning talent among the staff. You will want to be sure that they see helping you as serving their interests too.

Their assessment of you and your political team will evolve with accumulated experience in governing as you spend time together in the caucus and in the Cabinet room. They will get feedback from the backbenches of the team whether they seek it out or not. They will get discrete feedback from the Clerk of the Privy Council, who will be keeping a watchful eye on how ministers are performing and behaving, especially when the prime minister is not in the room.

Over the course of a mandate, ministers will rise or fall in the estimation of the PMO, and

> " Never forget that the PMO is fiercely loyal to the current prime minister and that if the staff feel threatened, they will attempt to cut potential threats down to size. "

how each minister is seen will change. Some of this assessment is out there for all to see and shows up in the occasional media scorecard. The PMO is keeping an eye on how well ministers perform when playing defence in Question Period or media scrums, how well they do when working the stakeholders and delivering the government's messages, whether they are useful on the circuit of pundit shows, and whether they are effective at generating a social media audience. Can a minister do it with ease in more than one language (if not English or French, how about Mandarin, Punjabi, or Cree)? Are you skilled at fundraising and political outreach for the party? These are the retail skills of being a minister that the PMO values highly.

What the media never see is the inside game, although they may scrape together bits of indirect feedback from "sources." More often than not, these sources are disgruntled with or hostile to the minister in question. Some ministers turn out to be solid, well prepared, and persuasive at the Cabinet table. Some not so much. A few key influencers will emerge. A few will turn out to be gifted at chairing meetings and will therefore be able to get committees and task teams to make decisions while keeping the team together. Some will be particularly good at cultivating the larger government caucus, picking up signs of potential trouble, and stoking morale and enthusiasm.

The PMO will be looking for good combinations (or pair bonds) of ministers with chiefs of staff and may decide that it needs to redeploy assets, perhaps by sending someone from its own team to help shore up a weakness or to fill an unplanned vacancy or perhaps by bringing in a talent that it needs on its own team. You may be expected to be a team player and cheerfully sacrifice one of your key players for the greater good. In the long run, it won't hurt to have someone at the "Centre" who knows a bit about you and your issues, so smile and move on.

Your Departure

Like death and taxes, and the firing of sports coaches, the end of a ministerial career is inevitable. Often, it will come with an election defeat for you and your team or more painfully with a defeat just for you and a few others. Or you may survive an election only to be sent to the Opposition benches. It takes a lot of dedication and perseverance to make the adjustment to life in Opposition once you have been a minister, and many cannot or will not.

Less frequently, you may be dropped from Cabinet between elections. You may have become a particularly vulnerable target, and the prime minister may conclude that the best way to cauterize the wound is to remove you quickly rather than holding out for a wider shuffle when you can be moved out of the line of fire. You can count on the prime minister to defend you – until the prime minister doesn't. Another reason why your time may be up is that there has been a change of leader and prime minister, and you don't fit into the new Cabinet choices.

These scenarios of involuntary departure unfold very quickly, sometimes in one day. They can be emotionally very turbulent times. People around you will feel protective of you, hurt and angry in some cases, and worried about their jobs in others. It can be hard on family, especially if you have been the quarry of a media wolf pack. For the senior civil servants around you, it can be a time of awkwardness, as they want to treat you well but are starting to think about the needs of your successor.

The least probable scenario for ending a ministerial career is that you leave at a time and in a manner of your own choosing.

The rules on conflict of interest make it all but impossible to test the waters of the job market. If an unsolicited offer comes in, you will have almost no time to accept it or turn it away. Report the contact to the ethics commissioner.

So there are two main scenarios for leaving under your own steam. You could let the prime minister or the prime minister's chief of staff know that you want to leave and try to agree on timing and perhaps flush out an appointment. In days past, appointments to the Senate or an ambassadorship were common tools for the prime minister to ease the departure of ministers. More recent prime ministers have been reluctant to use this method. The other scenario is to leave quickly, gambling that after you leave, you will have the time and space to look for something and that something will turn up. You may want to get started on running down the mandatory cooling off period, or get a jump on your colleagues. But you will tend to overestimate how marketable or valuable you are once you are no longer a minister. Some ex-ministers land well, but many do not.

Whatever the scenario, most ex-ministers will go through a difficult period of adjustment. Apart from the loss of amenities, such as a car and driver, and the loss of an attentive staff, with so many people being deferential and wanting your time, there will be an abrupt

> " People will remember how you treated them and especially how you made them feel, so keep that in mind as you pursue your time as minister. "

emptying-out of the schedule. People you used to see frequently will no longer contact you. There will be a psychological withdrawal from being in the arena, being part of a team, and having access to exclusive places, like the Cabinet room and the government lobby of the House of Commons.

There isn't much that you can do to prepare for this transition except to put some savings aside in order to tide you over and to be mindful from day one that your time as minister is finite. Remember that many of the people who are so deferential to you now won't care later. You are going to find out who your real friends are. People will remember how you treated them and especially how you made them feel, so keep that in mind as you pursue your time as minister.

5

ADVICE TO A
DEPUTY MINISTER

Deputy ministers (DMs) have a particular role in Westminster government, on top of their multifaceted challenges in leading and managing public sector institutions. There are variants in the United Kingdom (where they are called permanent secretaries) and Australia (where they are called departmental secretaries).

In Canada, their role has been set out in some detail in official documents, notably *Open and Accountable Government* and *Guidance for Deputy Ministers,* issued by the Privy Council Office. There is an excellent treatment of the evolution of the role over time in Jacques Bourgault's *The Deputy Minister's Role in the Government of Canada: His Responsibility and His Accountability* and in several other pieces that he has written over the years. (Half of the deputy ministers are women now, so

> " The appointment to any specific position is 'at pleasure,' which means that it can be revoked at any time and that there is no fixed tenure. "

future works will need new gender-neutral titles.)

There is a caricature of the deputy ministers as belonging to some sort of permanent priesthood, enduring while ministers and governments come and go. The television series *Yes Minister* did a lot to propagate this image of Sir Humphrey Appleby. The reality for any individual deputy minister is rather different. The appointment to any specific position is "at pleasure," which means that it can be revoked at any time and that there is no fixed tenure.

DMs are managed as a portfolio of assets, not just as individuals, and they may be redeployed to other positions or eased out altogether. One of the main roles of the clerk is to manage this portfolio and to leave it in better shape than when the clerk inherited it.

DMs tend to be appointed in their fifties, sometimes younger, and to leave in their sixties. Any given DM is probably going to stay in a job for somewhere between three and five years, which is probably going to overlap with more than one minister. Not many spend more than a decade in the DM ranks.

This overlap and turnover means that there is a constantly shifting set of pair bonds between ministers and deputy ministers.

TRANSITION PERIOD

Assigning and Moving Ministers

Generally, the decisions about assigning and moving ministers, whether at the start of a mandate or around "shuffles," are made by a very small group of people close to the prime minister. The prime minister's chief of staff and the clerk have the greatest influence, in part because they have proximity to the prime minister, whose trust they have earned, but also because between them they have the perspective on the whole portfolio of talent.

Fussing about Cabinet shuffles can go right to the last minute. In the final hours, the Privy Council Office will be seeking confirmation of a round of related decisions about the job title, whether to move any bits and pieces of government machinery at the same time, who will be the chief of staff and deputy minister for each minister on day one, which Cabinet committees the ministers should be assigned to, who will be formally assigned as the backup acting ministers in the event that ministers cannot perform their duties, and where they fit on the order of precedence (a list that a surprising number of people pay attention to).

The Privy Council Office also works with the Office of the Governor General to determine when and how the governor general will be involved, where a swearing-in ceremony will take place, how the necessary documents will be signed to give effect to the appointments, how many guests each minister can invite, whether the minister wants to swear an oath or an affirmation, and in which official language. All of these items will be decided while staff are trying to preserve secrecy around the event for as long as possible and political reporters are working to scoop their colleagues.

Getting the Call

At some point, the clerk will feel confident that the final shuffle is coming together and will call you as deputy minister in order to give you a bit of time to think about how to deal with the handover.

Naturally, if this is the start-up of a new Cabinet after an election, you will have had lots of time to get ready, and the date of the swearing-in will have been predicted with some degree of accuracy. Midway through the mandate, a shuffle can land on you suddenly, with only a day or two of heads-up, perhaps less. If your minister resigns for personal reasons, you might have been confided in and given some time to think ahead. The worst case is a sudden resignation, which can lead to a change of minister on the same day and a summons to Rideau Hall.

As a good deputy minister, you have continuously refreshed and stored away a core suite of onboarding material that can be warmed and served. You have already given some thought to a sequence of key briefings and events that can get the minister off and running, but you will have to be agile enough to adapt to the minister and to the circumstances, especially to the hot issues of the day, so your plan needs to be constructed in small modules. No transition planning calendar survives contact with reality, but it gives you a compass to move forward.

Dealing With Time Lags and Gaps

If the government is coming back from an election with a refreshed mandate or if it is shuffling ministers in the middle of one, there is often a time lag between moving ministers and moving their staff. The Prime Minister's Office will decide. Its interest is to avoid dropping the ball, or baton, in the hand-off, so it often asks the chief of staff or key personnel to stay where they are so that they can help to onboard a new minister or to drive a project to conclusion.

> As a good deputy minister, you have continuously refreshed and stored away a core suite of onboarding material that can be warmed and served.

Political staffers also accumulate expertise and experience in particular areas.

Your chief of staff may feel stranded between two canoes, eager to join the old minister somewhere else but needing to do a good job with the new one. The PMO may not have said whether the plan is for the chief of staff to move on, stay indefinitely, or leave the team. This job uncertainty can be very stressful when one is faced with little pension and minimal severance pay.

You may have to deal with a new chief of staff several weeks after the arrival of a new minister, changing the dynamics a second time.

If it is the start-up of a new government, you may go several weeks before a chief of staff arrives and before the minister's office is at full complement. The prime minister's transition team will have been scrambling to identify a roster of talent to recruit, some for the PMO itself and others to assign to around thirty ministers. It is a challenging puzzle for the team, and not all of those who are wanted may be willing or able to detach from their old lives and to relocate quickly. You will need to adjust and try to compensate for any early gaps in functions such as communications or parliamentary affairs.

Orientation and Guides

You are not alone in the start-up phase of a new minister. The PMO, with help from the PCO, always tries to organize orientation events for new ministers and for new political staff. The House of Commons organizes orientation and onboarding activities for new members of Parliament and for their families.

In recent years, each prime minister has issued and publicly posted a guide to the roles and expected conduct of people in government. *Open and Accountable Government* is a recent title. These handbooks have been lightly updated by new governments to reflect evolving aspects of governing and to enable them to put their own imprint on governance. The prime minister is likely to have emphasized and underscored some expectations in the mandate letter given to each minister.

All of these channels tend to reinforce a message that the minister should seek out and establish a strong working relationship with you, the deputy minister.

YOUR ROLE

The Confidence of the Minister

The main task of deputy ministers is to establish a solid working relationship with the ministers so that they can effectively discharge their responsibilities and accountabilities. The job of deputy ministers is to help ministers do their job. Part of your role as a deputy minister is to be a sort of executive coach. You will have some sense of the minister you have been given as a development project. Some are in the early days and full of potential, and you can help them to acquire a track record and skill set to advance. If they do, it will reflect well on you. Some have already settled in as steady performers or utility players and may not burn with ambition, at least not yet. (Every time a party leadership race opens up, we find out that all sorts of ministers have harboured thoughts of taking the big chair someday.) Others have established a track record as underperformers, and some will arrive battered and bruised from their previous assignment. Part of your task is to restore their confidence and help them to recover momentum and credibility. In these situations, the deputy minister is one of only a handful of people damaged ministers may open up to, but they may not. You will want to think about where your minister is situated and seek some insight from the clerk about how your minister is perceived by the "Centre."

Deputy ministers should aim to spend their time doing things that only deputy ministers get to do. Your most important task is to secure and maintain the trust and confidence of the minister. That doesn't mean telling ministers what they want to hear. On the contrary, you will want ministers to be confident that you will warn them of upcoming trouble and to trust you to give them frank advice and full information.

You don't have to be their friend or even to like them. It can happen, but it isn't necessary. You and your minister may be two people of very different backgrounds and temperaments thrown together like so many "buddy cop" partners. Whether you develop a professional camaraderie or not, it will help both of you to do your jobs if you develop a cordial and mutually respectful tone, especially in front of others. You should try to air out any serious disagreements or issues in private. The longer you stay together as a pair bond, the more likely you are to develop mutual respect and perhaps a real camaraderie, especially if you have been through some sort of crisis or ordeal together.

Chances are that you'll spend one to three years with ministers before they are moved or you are. Your start with a particular minister could be either you joining the minister or the

> " Your most important task is to secure and maintain the trust and confidence of the minister. "

minister joining you. Either way, the onus is on you to adapt to ministers, so you will need to quickly get a read on their way of learning and their way of getting to decisions. You may be able to call a colleague who has some previous experience with your minister and ask for tips.

There is no right way to be a minister, at least in the sense that each one is a distinct human. Some will be gregarious and talkative, and some will be quieter and reserved. Some love to read, and some prefer to talk and discuss. Some like to cross-examine and stress test until they are satisfied. Some give off few clues about what they really think or feel. Some are cautious and slow to reach decisions. Some are impulsive and reactive. Some can focus, and some are easily bored and distracted. Some bog down in minutiae, and some are strategic. Some are better in small groups of familiar people. You will have to figure out your minister and be an attentive observer.

You need to be realistic about the many other demands on ministers' time and help

> " ... the onus is on you to adapt to ministers ... "

them to make smart use of it. Do what you can to make sure that documents and briefings are concise and direct. Give them as much lead time and turnaround time as feasible so that they don't come to feel that everything is rushed and that they are at risk of something slipping by them. Keep an open dialogue going with the chief of staff about the cumulative pressures on the minister's schedule. Check in from time to time and ask ministers directly in private what is and isn't working for them.

Is Your Minister New or Experienced?
New ministers may have served as Opposition critics or House of Commons committee chairs and may have some familiarity with the port-folio – but not with being a minister. They may have served as provincial Cabinet ministers but are not familiar with the federal political eco-system or with the portfolio. Ministers of this last kind will arrive with expectations about their role, what kind of support they can expect, and how things work that may or may not align with Ottawa practice, but generally their past

experience can give them an early head start on their rookie colleagues.

Many of the new ministers in this category are also new to being a Member of Parliament, having just arrived in a general election or a by-election. Keep in mind the tremendous disruption of their lives that they are going through, their immediate preoccupation with family issues, their level of anxiety, and their culture shock. Keep an eye on the level of fatigue of someone just coming off an exhausting election campaign, and budget time for rest and recovery.

With ministers of this kind, you will want to spend a lot of time on the "how" of being a minister and what is likely to consume them – which will vary depending on whether yours is a portfolio that has large operations or regulatory functions, delivers front-counter services or funds other people, or perhaps combines some of these tasks.

They may turn to you for advice in the early days on how to be effective at Cabinet meetings or persuasive in the budget process. Or they may be overconfident, full of adrenalin, and charge on without you, and you may need to lean on your own relationships with the "Centre" in order to help your minister.

If your minister is experienced but new to your own portfolio, the advantage is that you

> " Reach out to the previous deputy minister and ask for tips on how the minister likes to work and whether there are particular go-to behaviours, preoccupations, or blind spots that you should know about. "

can fast-forward past a lot of the governance issues and get to talking through the specific issues in the portfolio. But you should be mindful that ministers will bring expectations and work habits based on their experience, both good and bad. So will their political staff if they came with the minister. Reach out to the previous deputy minister and ask for tips on how the minister likes to work and whether there are particular go-to behaviours, preoccupations, or blind spots that you should know about.

WORKING WITH THE MINISTER'S OFFICE

Avoiding Friction

Many working relationships with ministers and their offices run smoothly and productively. But sometimes friction can build between the department and the political office without you or the minister knowing. You need to be alert to how things are going and as open as possible with the chief of staff to defuse issues.

A common area of friction is timeliness. The minister's political staff will want the public servants in the department to respond quickly to their questions, to incoming correspondence, or to representations and inquiries that they have received from the PMO, other ministers' offices, and members of Parliament. They will want a buffer of time to see documents headed to the minister for signature and to play their role. They will want to participate in meetings and conference calls of the political network and to appear well informed and on top of the issues. They will need to be ready for cross-examination. These are reasonable demands, and you should try to factor their role into any timelines.

In portfolios with high volumes, the minister's political staff can easily come to feel "jammed" and start to grumble about the competence of the department. For its part, the department may be impatient to get the minister's signature in order to meet some external deadline, such as a tabling in Parliament or getting an item on a Cabinet or Treasury Board agenda. The department's key staff will quickly figure out whether certain members of the political office are disorganized or repeat offenders in falling behind, bottlenecking the flow, or even losing documents sent to them. Political staffers tend to live in the present, and few of them have habits and instincts for forward planning their work, however good they are at it.

It is essential to have good people working on the flow and acting as a bridge between the political staff and the public service. There will be someone in your department – either someone working in the deputy minister's office or someone who is styled as a department secretary – and someone in the minister's office who will act as either an office manager or an assistant to the chief of staff. Their ability to get along with each other, to use lists and tracking systems, and to spot and debug issues every day will minimize the number of issues that escalate to your attention or accumulate to damage relations. Don't take any of their work for granted. Check in regularly with your people, and don't hesitate to talk to the chief of staff.

Safety and Cybersecurity

One of the most important early conversations and briefings to have with the minister, and each staff member, is about personal safety and cybersecurity. Those who are new to the ministry or new to political life will likely be naive about the environment that they are now moving into and may feel that you are exaggerating the risks. Those who are coming from another department may be less innocent but will still need to become familiar with the particular threat and risk assessment and the protections that your portfolio offers, as well as with the specific networks and tools that they should be using to make their conversations, meetings, and documents as secure from interception as possible. You will want your departmental security officer to work with partners in order to create a secure zone that encompasses the minister's departmental office, parliamentary office, constituency office, car, and home, which may include a home back in the minister's constituency and a place in Ottawa.

All ministers, and all members of Parliament, are somewhat familiar with the torrent of abuse that is spewed on social media. Some will have had their first taste of it recently as candidates. Ministers have a higher profile and are associated with certain issues, so they will attract more sustained and more episodic abuse. Some more so than others. Ministers who are women, people of colour, Indigenous, or religious minorities will attract more haters.

New ministers are usually less familiar with the reality that for many of them their every conversation, meeting, email, and text is being targeted by several foreign intelligence services, who trawl constantly to see what turns up or who pursue specific people and topics. Ministers are in the middle of a never-ending race between interception capabilities and the Government of Canada's defences.

You should sit down early with the minister, the chief of staff, and the head of your security team and have a frank discussion. Sensitive and uncomfortable topics can be how much ministers will want to be informed about incoming personal threats, how much they will want to know about cyberbreaches, and how they will handle any lapses in good hygiene by staff. Some ministers will want to be very informed, whereas others will just want assurances that you will do what you can to protect them and that you will talk to the chief of staff as needed.

If you come to believe that the minister or one of the staff is being reckless with security issues, you must inform the clerk or the national security and intelligence adviser.

Tracking Document Flow

You will want to make sure that whatever system you have for tracking the flow of documents back and forth to the minister is sophisticated enough to tell what the minister has actually seen or read. Trust but verify. You have a very serious problem if you suspect that the political office is deliberately blocking information or advice from getting to the minister. The main reason why this interference could occur is that someone in the office wants the department to give different advice, more in line with what

> **"** You have a very serious problem if you suspect that the political office is deliberately blocking information or advice from getting to the minister. **"**

that person thinks is the right course, and tries to put pressure on the department to change its advice or to bury uncomfortable analysis. This conduct can create a game of "chicken" as a deadline looms or an issue builds in intensity.

The problem for you, as deputy minister, is that you are the accountable one in this relationship. The only "paper trail" that will show up in audits, production of documents for Access to Information requests or parliamentary questions, and production of documents in court cases for any of the officers of Parliament or for parliamentary committees, will be records that bear your signature or that of one of your public servants. The political office's advice is usually conveyed verbally, or through encrypted emails outside the government networks, or in a separate "grey note" that is highly unlikely to ever surface.

The role of political assistants is that of an invisible hand, and if they are ever put in the spotlight, their first instinct is usually avoidance: they will say either that they weren't told or that they were just following the information and advice that they were given by the department. If you bend advice to accommodate the political office, you won't be able to show that you had raised other options or considerations.

Avoiding this problem can be a real challenge. It isn't a simple black-and-white area of "truth to power." The staff of the political office may be right that the department has been timid or unimaginative. They may be right that the officials are out of touch with how an issue is seen or how an initiative is likely to be received. They may be right that the department's advice is full of various forms of unconscious bias.

The structural imbalance is that political offices tend to underestimate implementation risks and costs and to be impatient about timelines, whereas departments tend to be overly cautious and are likely to go to what they are familiar with as a solution.

To avoid this imbalance becoming a serious problem, you will need to keep working at creating space and time for candid exchange back and forth. Remind the staff of the political office that they always have the option to convey their views through a covering note of their own. Don't ever sign or send anything that you aren't comfortable with. If you think that your advice

> Don't ever sign or send anything that you aren't comfortable with.

or important information is being filtered or blocked, raise it privately with the chief of staff and if necessary with the minister. You may be able to fire a warning shot by referring to a previous note during a briefing that you suspect didn't get through.

Avoiding Political Interference

In addition to tussles about policy advice, there can be a constant temptation by political staff to get involved in the department's day-to-day business. Allocations from funding programs, procurement processes, and regulatory approvals are recurrent themes where there is potential friction. Delaying or suppressing the release of reports and other information can become a serious source of contention. Some ministers' offices have been known to insist that the minister have final sign-off on travel and conference attendance by public servants, which gives the political office line of sight to departmental business when the requests for approval come in, creating a choke point for them to exercise leverage.

You may need to push back from time to time and remind the chief of staff or the minister of the danger to be faced if the minister is caught out in "political interference." Political staff will insist that the minister is accountable and has a right to be involved.

Blatant interference for partisan reasons, such as directing a grant or contract to others because they are allies or donors, even though they may be unqualified, is rare these days. There is too much transparency related to funding programs and procurement processes for it to go undetected. Pressure directed toward ministers and their staff is more about convincing them that they need to create or modify a program, or that the government really needs to acquire something that someone is selling, or that the government should approve the use of something in Canada (or make sure it can still be used). This kind of pressure is directed at getting the design and specifications of spending programs or procurements bent to increase the chances that the lobbying group or firm will come out on top.

"Interference" essentially comes down to a program or process varying too far from the way that Canadians were told that it was supposed to work. If the outcomes were different or the process was different from what someone can find on the program's website, the discrepancy will stand out and be noticed.

Try to establish a safe zone to discuss with the minister and staff the stated goals, the design, the eligibility criteria, the weighting of factors, the steps in the process, and the timelines, and be open to feedback. Giving the minister some sense of shared ownership will make it easier to stand your ground on specific cases.

Communications

The area of greatest day-to-day stress in the relationship between the department and the minister is almost certainly going to be communications. The interests and perspectives of the department and its agencies in communications are never perfectly aligned with the interests of the minister's office. Nor are the skill sets.

Ministers have, or quickly gain, exposure to being on the spot as the spokesperson, which requires trying to fit messaging into tiny packets of time afforded by Question Period answers, scrums, interviews, and social media posts. They may have spent time as a Member of Parliament or an Opposition critic. They seek simplicity in phrasing, a "killer fact," an anecdote, or a metaphor. They know that their opponents are doing the same, and they know that it is much easier to attack than to defend, but they have to play defence most of the time.

The department will tend to want to tell a more complicated story reinforced by context and bolstered with facts. It is psychologically vested in the way that things are or in wanting to see something through. In contrast, a minister's office is quicker to cut and run. It has a greater willingness to retreat from or to abandon an initiative in order to make the pain go away.

The political staff have a default setting that is responsive, bordering on hyperactive, and they highly value speed. They will scan and see danger coming in from conventional and social media – and be jumpy and reactive. They will want concise responses that can rebut arguments or correct facts. They will also see opportunities to try to get on the front foot and will have core messages that the minister can deploy in media scrums, in interviews, and on panel shows or that staff can post on social media. Someone in the minister's office has to sit in on a very early morning conference call chaired by the PMO that serves as the government's political radar for the coming day and starts a process of refreshing responsive "media lines" for use, if needed, by other ministers and the government caucus.

The PMO's communications team will see your minister as just one asset to be deployed for the team. For responsive purposes, the minister may be instructed to appear on one or more of the pundit and panel shows, or to go out and offer journalists a "scrum," or to issue a statement. For proactive purposes, the PMO will have sorted out air traffic control and decided which ministers will make what announcements on which day. Your minister may be tapped to serve as a supporting player because of second-language skills or due to a profile with regional or "ethnic" media. All of these tasks eat into the minister's calendar and create fresh deadlines to be ready.

There will be opportunities for the minister to deliver a longer-form message – perhaps as a speech in parliamentary debate or before an audience at a stakeholder event or an international conference. Ministers vary in their ability to give speeches and in their preferences, so finding a writer who can deliver an acceptable draft can be a challenge. Speeches are a "just in time delivery" business. People will tend to focus on them only close to a deadline, and by the time drafts have been passed around for fact-checking or input, that deadline is likely close at hand. And the draft is likely to read like it was written by a committee. Someone who can perk up a speech at the last minute is incredibly valuable.

Much of the time, communications is about playing good defence. On any given day, there can be something to respond to. Editors and producers have to fill their pages and their shows with something, so if a report or statement is released by a stakeholder, if a study is

> " Much of the time, communications is about playing good defence. "

posted by a think tank or academic, or if one of the more than a dozen institutional watchdogs tables a report card or findings, it will be "newsworthy," which will feed the Opposition, whose members will provide a round of reaction to feed another cycle. Most of the time, this cycle will last two days, perhaps three, unless something gives it fresh kindling or oxygen. Communications is often like a fire sprinkler system putting out sparks. If you are in the third day of a story, you are in trouble, and it will take a much greater effort to make it go away.

If ministers are really unfortunate, they will become the focus of the entire media pack for a while, and scarce journalistic resources will be allocated to digging up new angles in order to keep the story going. A typical cycle is that once a story has broken, stakeholders, journalists, and Opposition staff immediately file a raft of requests under tools such as Access to Information legislation or written questions in Parliament, hoping to peel the onion further.

If you are really fortunate, the media will become focused on someone else's minister, distracting attention from yours, but don't assume that they won't return. If your minister is the piñata of choice, your communications shop will be taken into a form of receivership by the "Centre" – the PMO and the PCO – whose staff will direct the efforts to manage the issue and get back on track.

The elusive goal in communications, never quite reached, is to be proactive, bending media coverage to have to respond to actions by the government and driving some sort of "strategy." The "comms plan" for your minister might be about a significant initiative such as a new piece of legislation or launching a new program. Or it could be about supporting the government's broader approach to a theme. Good communications plans anticipate probable reactions across a range of stakeholders and segments of the public, shaping a series of "announceables" with accompanying messaging. Successful strategies require persistence and repetition over time in order to sustain momentum, overcome resistance, and battle a tendency to lose focus and drift back to reactive mode.

The department's communications shop will have some strengths. Most issues have a long history, and their path is dependent on what has occurred in the past. Even a genuine shock will soon be compared to how something similar was handled. The department

> " The elusive goal in communications, never quite reached, is to be pro- active, bending media coverage to have to respond to actions by the government and driving some sort of 'strategy.' "

may be able to quickly identify these patterns and may be familiar with and able to anticipate the behaviour of some of the stakeholders and journalists. It can draw on internal resources who understand the issue and know what evidence is available to support both defence and offence. What the minister's communications team will be better at than the department is taking content and then calibrating tone, adding edge, and including an appropriate element of counterattack.

It will be very difficult to build up any kind of narrative around the cumulative record of the minister or the government in any particular area. Your minister or your department will regularly be accused of having accomplished nothing. It is never easy to put into context whatever is consuming communications in the present. The media and social media have short attention spans and are hyperfocused on what is happening and on what people are saying today. Nevertheless, it is worth the effort to make sure that your department is constantly stocking and posting material – such as backgrounders, maps, lists, trackers, activity reports, and videos. Make sure that information is bite-sized, in plain language, and easily shareable on social media.

REASSIGNMENT

Starting Up with a New Minister

The relationship between a deputy minister and a minister is not balanced. If the relationship breaks down – if it falls below some basic level of trust and confidence – it is rarely recoverable. It is the deputy minister who is likely to be moved.

If you do have to start up with a new minister from the same government after a shuffle, much may depend on the circumstances that led to the departure of the last one. If the previous minister was moved up or sideways, the incoming minister is likely to see you as someone who must have been helpful. If the previous minister was removed from the line of fire or moved to cauterize a crisis, the incoming minister may have some unspoken worry that you were part of the mess, and you will have to work a bit harder to gain this person's confidence.

After a change of government, many ministers and their teams instinctively feel uncomfortable dealing with someone they know was working with their predecessor from the other side not that long ago. It can take weeks or months for this wariness to ease. Sometimes, it never does.

There isn't much that you can do other than carry on and show that you are competent and useful. Be mindful of language. You and your people may have unconsciously picked up jargon and terminology used by the previous government that can be jarring to the new minister – who may interpret attempts to explain background and context as defensiveness. Nonetheless, you should never be tempted to speak ill of the previous government or minister or seem overly eager to please. That is likely to backfire by reducing confidence in you. The new minister will start to worry that you will do the same when the new minister has moved on. It is more important to earn respect than to be liked. Holding back key information is a sure-fire way to lose the Minister's trust.

Some ministers give off clear signs of impending trouble. They become harder to get time with, they stop reaching out to you, or they start having more meetings where you are not invited. They begin to call directly into the department to talk to people lower down the chain of command without letting you know.

> If you sense that you have not clicked with your minister or that you are entering a red zone, the best course is to try to air it out privately with the minister.

If you sense that you have not clicked with your minister or that you are entering a red zone, the best course is to try to air it out privately with the minister. Most relationships are recoverable. The surest way is to get things done together. If your judgment is that the situation with the minister is becoming untenable, let the clerk know while there is still time to do something. The clerk may have a sense that you can hold out until the next Cabinet shuffle or may intervene with the minister directly to try to repair the situation. The clerk may be able to help patch things up, give you some useful feedback or advice, or if necessary create an exit strategy for you. You may be well suited to another assignment with a different minister. Part of the clerk's concern is to look for good pair bonds.

Handling a Minister's Exit
A ministerial career can end through election defeat or shuffle, sometimes through political

crisis or scandal, and occasionally through death or illness. As deputy minister, you play a distinct role in the hand-off from one minister to the next, and the more challenging part of the hand-off can be the exit of the outgoing minister. Outgoing ministers retain all of their authorities and accountabilities until they are formally transferred to someone else – who could be the pre-named acting minister for a short period of time or a successor. You have a formal role in securing and archiving the records of the outgoing Minister.

The scenarios for exit create very different psychological and emotional conditions. If the whole team was defeated, the minister may be crossing over into Opposition and will be accompanied by familiar faces. Thoughts may even be turning to an impending leadership race. It can be a bitter pill if the team was reelected but your minister's seat was lost or your minister was not chosen for the new Cabinet. The minister will likely be in considerable turmoil about what comes next and about how this turn of events affects income and pension, family, and where to live. The last thing on the minister's mind may be dealing with any sputtering bits of departmental business, so you will want to triage ruthlessly and hold back what you can. In a sudden departure, the minister may be angry or tearful and still the target of media interest and pundit speculation. The

> " Make sure that you have assigned a 'concierge' to handle personnel and logistical matters with empathy. "

minister may have been cut off or frozen out by the prime minister's team and feel very isolated and vulnerable.

Whatever the scenario, life for an ex-minister can suddenly become very lonely. This is a time when you should step up and ensure that the minister and the political staff are treated with respect and care. Your team may be overeager to impress the incoming minister and clumsily start changing signage and websites, asking for the return of computers and phones, or re-assigning the car and driver. These things can be bruising to the minister and especially to the political staff, who are probably very anxious. Make sure that you have assigned a "concierge" to handle personnel and logistical matters with empathy.

Unless it is impossible in the circumstances, make sure that there is some moment or gesture of acknowledgment of every minister's tenure, however long or short it was. Host a gathering, whether it is small or large. Arrange for photos and mementoes, preferably something that speaks to the portfolio. Offer to take the minister and chief of staff out to dinner. Not only is this attention the right thing to do, but it will also affect the minister's views and perceptions of you, the department, and the public service for many years to come – and what the minister tells others. Ministers may reappear years later in politics or in another walk of life, and they will remember how you made them feel.

6

LOOKING TO THE FUTURE

As it has in the past, I have no doubt that the tradecraft of governing will adapt and evolve. A modern prime minister has to deal with social media platforms and a deluge of information that would have confounded predecessors.

But some aspects are likely to be enduring. Canada, provided it continues to fend off secession of any of its parts, which I am confident it will, is likely to still work with the same core institutional software. The people who govern Canada will be working with a Westminster model of parliamentary democracy, a federation, and the constraints of the Constitution, especially the division of powers and the Charter.

THE CONSTITUTIONAL IMPASSE

Although it is the playground of academics and op-ed writers, there is little chance that the fundamental institutions will change. Canada's constitution is all but impossible to amend; it is locked down, and new locks were added after the three unsuccessful rounds of negotiation in the 1980s and 1990s. One has to construct a scenario in which a constitutional amendment would be agreed to by the federal Parliament and all ten provinces, several of which now require a plebiscite before their legislature can ratify. Furthermore, although not formally required, it would be difficult to refuse to submit the amendments to a national referendum along the lines of the Charlottetown Accord, defeated in October 1992, and referenda are more likely to reject than approve.

The legal and political reality in Canada is that some form of consent by Indigenous peoples would be required in order to make fundamental changes to the institutions of government. What is less clear is how this consent would be secured, from whom, and where in the process.

The other challenge is that pursuing any one line of constitutional reform automatically leads to demands to deal with other issues, and this situation creates an expansion of bargaining: I'll support you on that, if you support me on this. From the perspective of a federal prime minister, opening up any aspect of constitutional reform will invite the war of all against all.

So the scope for institutional change is likely to be confined to nonconstitutional changes – to the processes that select the key actors without changing their basic role. Perhaps a different way to pick a governor general? Perhaps a different voting system to choose members of Parliament? But given that voters have rejected change in plebiscites in British Columbia (2005, 2009, 2018), Ontario (2017), and Prince Edward Island (2005, 2016), the prospects that any alternative will emerge as a consensus and be approved by a national referendum seem dim.

Future governments may change the way that senators are selected before being appointed, giving more say to the premiers or reverting to a more closed process for identifying candidates, or they may put in place different ways to drum up and screen candidates.

COALITIONS AND CONFIDENCE PACTS

As long as Canada uses a "first past the post" electoral system, there is going to be a tendency for majority governments to emerge. But the addition of third and fourth parties can lead to very close outcomes in seats or to situations where the largest party does not hold a majority of seats in the House. Parties with a strong regional base, like the Bloc Québécois or the Reform Party of the 1990s, can harvest enough seats to make the arithmetic of anyone else reaching a majority difficult.

Canada has lots of experience with minority government. The prime minister may simply choose to proceed for as long as possible, working on each confidence vote in the House as a separate test and working with any of the other parties to secure the necessary margin. This approach puts a premium on tactical adjustments, negotiating skills, and personal relationships. The government House leader may be a key player in keeping the show on the road.

The other option for an incoming prime minister is to seek greater stability and predictability by negotiating a more lasting accommodation with one of the other parties. This pact will allow the government to pass key measures that demonstrate that it retains the confidence of the House – notably the budget and supply (or appropriation of funding). Several provincial governments have successfully used a formal and very public "confidence pact" to get through a couple of years. In other cases, a less formal political understanding can be developed.

Some future prime ministers and ministers are going to find themselves facing the additional challenges and constraints of minority government or formal confidence pacts, which will mostly translate into anticipating the reaction of the other parties and working it into government initiatives.

What we have not seen for a century (since the First World War) is a coalition government – one where ministers are named from more than one political party. A coalition is a big step not only in sharing power but also in sharing accountability and the disciplines of Cabinet solidarity. There is no reason why Westminster can't accommodate coalition governments; we have seen them in the United Kingdom, Australia, New Zealand, and Ireland. Other European systems almost always produce coalition governments, so the potential partnerships and alliances among political parties are anticipated and discussed during each election campaign.

It seems likely that someday a provincial or federal election in Canada will produce a formal coalition government again. Most of what has been set out in this book will still apply. Experience in other countries suggests that it may be a greater strain on the smaller party that agrees to sign on and join the government. This party would be gambling that having influence, acquiring government experience, and advancing at least some of its priorities would be rewarded in the long run. However, it would be taking a lot of risks: it would share blame if the government turns out to be unpopular, or conversely the other party could get most of the credit at the next election. For the other parties, it may be easier to stay out of government, retain enough distance to be critical, and bargain for specific measures.

THE RISING COST OF POLITICAL LIFE

Political life has always meant accepting a certain degree of public visibility and a lot of criticism from strangers. Although rare in Canada compared to many other countries, there have been episodes of violence directed at politicians and the places where they work.

The spread of social media platforms seems to be adding a new dimension – anonymous abuse and threats directed not just at politicians but also at their family members, their staff, and their public servants. Greater attention has to be paid to personal security, and it is a challenge for protective services to sift out the harmless crank from the killer.

Women in politics bear an extra burden of misogynist abuse, and many forms of racism and bigotry blight the social media landscape. This situation isn't unique to politics, but the cost of participating in public life is rising. For some, it will no longer be worth it. We will find out soon whether it is going to deter people from entering politics or shorten the duration that they are willing to stay. Over time, will it change the pool of people from which the leaders discussed in this book will emerge?

INDIGENOUS RECONCILIATION

Every prime minister of the past several decades has made an attempt to change the trajectory of outcomes of Canada's Indigenous peoples. Some came to a strong personal commitment later in their tenure, and others did so early on. Some governments were pushed there by the courts, like it or not, as judges gave shape to the rights recognized in the Charter in 1982.

A full treatment is well beyond this book, but it seems likely that in the 2020s and beyond, prime ministers and an increasingly broad array of ministers will be spending more time working on the federal government's relationship with Indigenous peoples – a relationship that is actually seen by many as one with the Crown or as a nation-to-nation relationship. What this relationship means in practice is going to be a challenge for all future governments.

For the executive functions of government, the law is already shaping practice. The courts have created jurisprudence regarding the honour of the Crown and a duty by the Crown to consult Indigenous rights holders and to accommodate them that will reverberate for years to come.

One of the unresolved issues ahead will be how the legislative functions of government may be affected. Parliament is already constrained because a court may strike down legislative provisions that it finds infringe on constitutional protections, but that happens after the fact. Indigenous leaders are going to call for greater input into the process of developing legislation before it is adopted and will try to expand their ability to block initiatives. The courts are likely to be invited to rule on whether the duty to consult applies to legislatures and not just to the executive.

For the government, where Indigenous peoples fit in will not be straightforward. Some entities are the actual rights holders that the Crown is obliged to deal with, or they will assert that they are. Others are essentially advocacy organizations representing the interests of national, provincial, or regional aggregations of communities. Some will claim to speak for the large share of Indigenous peoples who do not live on reserves or the land bases of the self-governing nations, but rather in the cities and towns of Canada.

Should the federal government treat the Indigenous political organizations as governments and invite them to meetings with provincial and territorial governments? If so, which ones – all meetings or some for specific agenda items? Provincial governments have not been unanimous about what the rules of engagement are. Or are the Indigenous organizations important "stakeholders" that should be there when broader issues are discussed? Should there be a specific process for engaging them set out in some sort of protocol? Or all of the above? At the end of the day, how much legal or political leverage will Indigenous organizations have on Cabinets and legislatures? Some Indigenous individuals will find themselves members of those Cabinets and legislatures, trying to influence their colleagues and nudge along outcomes, but they will be subject to all the disciplines of Cabinet and caucus unity.

Working through how Indigenous peoples fit into the Westminster model and into the federation is likely to be one of the dominant issues in Canadian governance in the next couple of decades.

TECHNOLOGY

Practices within Canadian government have already been affected and disrupted by the arrival of new technologies. Much has been said about politicians embracing Twitter, Facebook, and other tools to get their messages across and about how televising Question Period and parliamentary committees has changed behaviours and the role of the media as an intermediary. Yet the core "software" of Westminster described in this book hasn't really changed. Will there be greater disruption in years to come?

More recent innovations have increased the potential for many of the deliberative processes to move to online platforms, freeing members of Parliament and ministers from the need to physically be in the Cabinet room or House of Commons. This change will give them more options about where to be and how to use their time. There will be interest in adding a form of electronic voting that reduces even further the slivers of time needed for parliamentary votes. Cabinet and its committees already function with ministers calling in from distant locations, without jeopardizing Cabinet confidentiality or the availability of simultaneous interpretation.

This reduction in the importance of proximity to Parliament Hill isn't going to make life easier for ministers. They are still bound by the limits of the 168-hour week, but there will be more pressures on the use of these hours. It will be more difficult to say no to invitations. Their calendars will fill up as surely as an additional lane on a commuter highway is soon filled with cars.

An interesting choice may lie ahead. Even before the COVID-19 pandemic, there was pressure to add online voting to the options for general elections. The main obstacle now is that the danger of hacking and cyberattacks exceeds any perceived benefit. But if this problem is eventually resolved and other countries demonstrate that it can work, should Canadians be able to vote for their local Member of Parliament by spending a few minutes on their laptop or phone?

It isn't really an issue of accessibility. Given the availability of mail-in and proxy voting and the generous provisions for advance voting, I argue that there is still something important about joining other members of the local community at a gathering place and casting a ballot.

Living in a peaceful society under the rule of law and being able to participate in a democratic exercise of citizenship and community should never be treated as banal or routine. It should require some mindful effort once every few years to remind us what we have built here.

In the end, however the tradecraft of governing Canada evolves, the most important thing will always be that we retain the ability to choose the small group of Canadians who get to practise it and the ability to change them from time to time.

ACKNOWLEDGMENTS

Although much of this book draws on my first-hand experience, I have to recognize that it was influenced by colleagues, bosses, and mentors who gave me the extraordinary opportunities that shaped my public service career, and I thank the support staff and teams that made everything possible. I want to give a special shout-out to the politicians and to their political staff, who also serve Canada. You all enriched my journey and taught me so much. In the end, for me, as it is for all the people I have written about, it is my family that deserves the last word. I cannot find the right ones to express my gratitude and love.